Altered Books,
Collaborative Journals,
and Other Adventures in Bookmaking

ROCKPORT

Altered Books,
Collaborative Journals,
and Other Adventures in Bookmaking

GLOUCESTER MASSACHUSETTS

ROCKPORT PUBLISHERS

HOLLY HARRISON

First published in the United States of America by

Rockport Publishers, Inc.
33 Commercial Street
Gloucester, Massachusetts 01930-5089
Telephone: (978) 282-9590
Fax: (978) 283-2742
www.rockpub.com

Library of Congress Cataloging-in-Publication Data
Harrison, Holly.
     Altered books, collaborative journals, and other adventures in
     bookmaking / Holly Harrison.
             p.   cm.
     Includes bibliographical references.
     ISBN 1-56496-995-9 (pbk.)
     1. Altered books. I. Title.
     TT896.3.H37 2003
     702'.8'1—dc21   2003002176

10 9 8 7

Design: Susan Raymond

Layout: Chebacco Design & Communications, LLC

Copyeditor: Sarah T. Chaffee

All photography by Bobbie Bush, www.bobbiebush.com, except where indicated and on the following pages: 88-90, 94-95, 96-97, 99-101, 106, and 113-115.

Printed in Singapore

window

Contents

*Preceding page: Hybrid tea fragr
cloud. Battlefields blossomed with*

FLOWER OF D

Where blood was spille

ANY bloody battlefie

When starting this project, I was familiar with art journals and artist books but had seen only a few contemporary altered books. As a writer and lover of books, I found the idea both fascinating

Getting Started

and slightly appalling. Cut up a book? Paint on the pages? But I quickly found that altered book artists are true book enthusiasts. If anything, they are more passionate about books than many readers: They want to climb inside and interact with what's on the page. As I did my research, I never stopped marveling at the inventiveness and artistry involved in the making of books, the dreaming up of new forms, and book altering. I hope you'll enjoy the journey as much as I have.

—*Holly Harrison*

▲ An altered page created by Suz Simanaitis in an old copy of *Alice in Wonderland*.

Hands down, the most common advice offered by altered book artists is to have fun and forget about following rules. However, here are a few guidelines to keep in mind (or not) as you think about your first project.

Choosing a Book

• **Size:** The thicker the book, the more pages to deal with—either by removing or altering them. *War and Peace* is probably not a good candidate, but a children's board book or a slim volume of poems could be just right.

• **Paper quality:** Cheap paper won't stand up to abuse. You'll be investing a lot of time in your book, so choose one that will last.

• **Price:** You might find it easier to cut up a book that's inexpensive or free. Shop at flea markets, yard sales, and thrift stores, or rescue discarded books and covers at binderies. For specific book ideas, see page 12.

Basic Supplies

While some materials are suggested on the project pages, you'll also need to have these items at hand: artist brushes, a craft knife and self-healing cutting mat (for cutting windows and niches), scissors, pens, pencils, erasers, a ruler, a burnishing tool (a bone folder or an old credit card) for smoothing glued pages and creasing folds, waxed paper, and newspapers to protect your work surface.

Adhesives

Acid-free glues, such as PVA or archival glue sticks, dry clear and won't stain as they age. Acrylic mediums dry clear and are easy to use, however, some artists advise against them because they can cause pages to stick. Avoid rubber cement: It dries out over time and loses its ability to hold.

PROTECTING PAGES

Collaged pages and those painted with acrylics can stick together. One remedy is to put waxed paper between pages until they are fully dry. Another is to use a clear spray sealer such as Krylon Crystal Clear (available in art supply and craft stores) or a wax product such as Renaissance Wax (available at photo supply stores). These products can subtly alter the surface, so experiment to find out what works best for you.

Chapter One

Altered Books

Altering books has become increasingly popular over the past few years, with societies of book artists forming, artist Web sites springing up on the Internet, and galleries mounting exhibits. Although connected to rubber-stamping, collage, and the making of artist books, altered books are coming into their own. Artists are adapting techniques from other media, discovering new materials, and developing a multimedia approach that's uniquely theirs, adding flaps and cutting windows to conceal and reveal images, creating niches and shrine-like areas, and painting, collaging, abrading, and burning pages to produce a wide range of effects.

What is it about the nature of books that makes altering them such fun? Because "fun" is the operative word when artists talk about this medium. "It seems more playful than, say, if you're doing a traditional painting or collage or something that you're putting all of this 'serious art thought' into," says Sarah Fishburn. "Maybe it's because we're messing around with somebody else's creation, and it feels not just playful but maybe a tad naughty." Of course, we were all told not to color in our books when we were children—and here's an art form that actually encourages it. It's a little subversive, really.

A great benefit to working in books is that they are portable: You can easily take them on vacation, to a café, or to a friend's house. Another advantage is that a printed book already has something on the page, which can be less intimidating than confronting a blank piece of paper or canvas. There's something there for the artist to react to, whether it's by highlighting words to form a new narrative or painting washes of color over the text to create a background for new art.

Finally, altering a book provides the opportunity to develop a body of work. "It's really like working in a series because it's one whole piece of work," explains Michelle Ward. "Because you're driven by the book, driven by the theme, driven by the text, driven by the images, you can really develop a story of images across your pages. You can develop what your images are or what your colors are or what you're telling by pulling out the text." A collage or painting is just one piece, whereas an altered book is an instant series.

By experimenting with a variety of materials and book formats, the artists in this chapter overlay their own narratives onto a book, whether it's a novel, an old photo album, or a dictionary. However you decide to proceed, the main thing is that you do: Find a book, gather some art supplies, forget those grammar school rules, and dig in.

WHAT ABOUT COPYRIGHT?

Admittedly, there are some concerns, especially for artists hoping to publish their work. In a collage, it is fairly easy to transform found papers so they are no longer recognizable. But with a whole book, that's harder to do. If you want to play it safe, stick to volumes in the public domain—those published before 1923 or between 1923 and 1967 with no copyright renewal. (You can research this on the Internet.) For an excellent discussion of copyright concerns, see *dog eared magazine*, issue 3, summer 2001.

• **Address Books.** Instead of tossing out old address books, paint and collage the pages, letting familiar names and your handwriting add character. Or seek out vintage ones at flea markets, and paste in sepia photographs and found papers.

• **Children's Books.** Board books, pop-up books, storybooks, comic books, foam books, cloth books, fairy tales, and other volumes intended for children are all fair game for your own playtime.

Some Books to Play With

Keep in mind that a volume's size affects the size of your work area as well as the character of the final piece. Smaller books allow for a more intimate feeling, whereas larger ones offer room for bold expression. Also consider how the book's character will infuse the artwork. An embossed leather cover conveys an aura of history, whereas a children's board book has an inherently playful quality.

• **Coffee-Table Books.** The beautiful paper and photography of a coffee-table book will ensure that your artwork will last, which is no small matter when you spend many months working on a project.

• **Dictionaries.** Reference books can be effective springboards for your art. Highlight words with paint or colored pens and scatter related images across your page. Paint or collage over blocks of words to create places where the eye can rest.

• **Old Atlases.** The nostalgic nature of old maps may inspire you to create a personal or political history. Or rename the countries and give them funky colors.

• **Phone Books.** Let your fingers do the walking through discarded Yellow Pages, ripping and tearing, gluing, taping, sewing, cutting windows, drilling holes, and adding layers of paint and paper.

• **Pulp Fiction.** Old detective fiction often has fabulously retro covers that could prompt a walk on the campy side. Lighten up the sinister storylines with a new narrative or indulge in the darkest of fantasies.

• **Romance Novels.** The goofy covers and stilted dialogue of 1970s romance novels are just begging to be altered. Rewrite the stories from a feminist perspective, indulge in romantic cynicism, or transform a clichéd ending with surreal images.

• **Textbooks.** These have sturdy bindings and are often filled with drawings or illustrations that can add visual punch to your artwork. Revamp a medical text as a narrative on matters of the heart or use a geography book as a travel journal (for journeys real and imagined).

• **Vintage Books.** Many books printed in the late 1800s or early 1900s have beautiful covers but extremely fragile pages. Gut a book and fill it with handmade paper or found papers to create a unique venue for journaling and artwork. Tip: Avoid valuable collector's items and first editions!

• **Your Favorite Novel.** Because book altering necessitates a bigger time commitment than drawing a picture or making a single collage, consider working in a book you already love. That way, as you confront its pages over time, you'll keep finding inspiration.

▲ Altered dictionary pages by Melissa McCobb Hubbell.

Become Me

Brenda Murray

The following spreads are from an altered book by Brenda Murray, who was inspired by Tom Phillips's A Humument *(a 367-page Victorian novel he altered in the 1970s, highlighting words to create his own narrative). Murray reduced her book to 35 spreads by cutting out pages and gluing the end pages together. Instead of planning a cohesive story, she chose pages at random, recasting text by highlighting some words and obscuring the rest with paint and collage. The transformed spreads are linked visually and thematically, focusing on values important to her: love, honor, trust, respect, home, friends, and family.*

MATERIALS assorted paper scraps and ephemera • found objects and embellishments • acrylic paints • bought and hand-carved stamps • makeup sponge • needle and waxed linen bookbinding thread • PVA glue • basic supplies (see page 9)

Photography: Marie Frechon

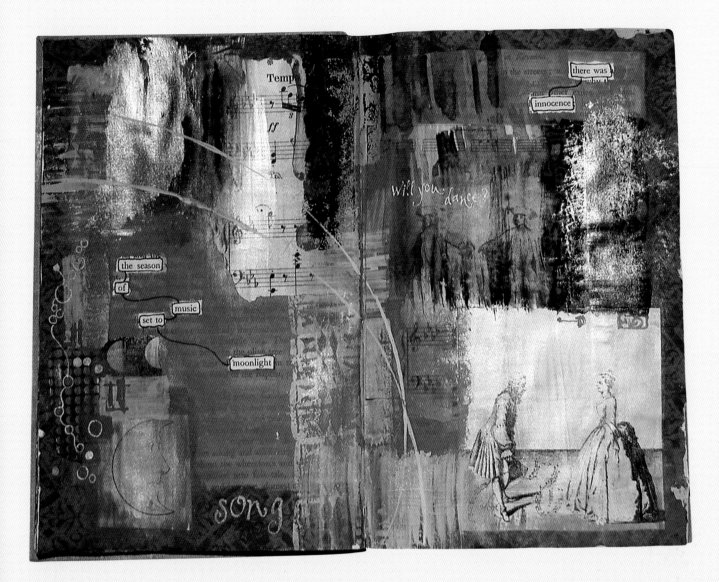

Brenda Murray on altered books and collage

"My altered books are different from collage because I'm working with words that are already there on the page. The boundaries set by the text are what make it interesting and challenging. I use a lot of text in my collage work, but it's different because it's things I choose—I'm making the story. With altered books, depending on the mood you're in or the kind of person you are or what's important to you, you can and will find a story. So the possibilities are endless."

◄ **Stitching, Beading, and Objects** A playful musing on the number 35, this page employs Murray's signature style in a palette dominated by greens, yellows, and reds. A distinctive feature is the stitching, which she added by punching holes through a block of pages (about 24) and then using bookbinding thread and a blanket stitch to attach glass beads. The domino is a real one; Murray carved a space for it and glued it in place before sewing the pages together.

▼ **Layering** Deep red and gold set a rich tone for this spread, which reflects on the paradoxical nature of love. The artist stamped a maze-like pattern for a background, then added layers of stamped and collaged images. At bottom right, a flush-faced woman plays self-consciously with her hair, gazing off the page, perhaps at the object of her affection.

▲ Expressing a Mood Like the emotion expressed, this spread is direct and spare: A single color dominates the canvas, and a smattering of details tells the story. The word "need" hovers in one corner, an envelope fills another (it contains a note and a ticket), and handwritten text, presumably a love letter, peeks out from behind the woman.

▶ Playing with Meanings A playful collaged harlequin juggles puzzle pieces under an orange found-paper moon (a depiction of an astronomer's instrument). There is something magical in the air, a sense that anything is possible. A whimsical pun in the text, a play on "piece" and "peace," further enhances the mood and shows the artist's delight in discovering hidden meanings in the text.

Technique Highlight:

LAYING OUT A PAGE

▼ **Highlighting Text** When creating a new text, Brenda Murray thinks visually: "Usually I'll decide, 'Now I'd like to do a spread that has my text in the upper left-hand side,' so I'll concentrate there and see what leaps out. You have to keep in mind that those highlighted words are the foundation for the structure of your page." The examples show two treatments of the same paragraph; each one moves the eye in a different way across the page.

linen is scorched, the roast burns, chinaware gets broken; these are absolute disasters, for when things are destroyed, they are gone forever. Permanence and security cannot possibly be obtained through them. The pillage and bombs of war threaten one's wardrobes, one's house.

The products of domestic work, then, must necessarily be consumed; a continual renunciation is required of the woman whose operations are completed only in their destruction. For her to acquiesce without regret, these minor holocausts must at least be reflected in someone's joy or pleasure. But since the housekeeper's labor is expended to maintain the *status quo*, the husband, coming into the house, may notice disorder or negligence, but it seems to him that order and neatness come of their own accord. He has a more positive interest in a good meal. The cook's moment of triumph arrives when she puts a successful dish on the table: husband and children receive it with warm approval, not only in words, but by consuming it gleefully. The culinary alchemy then pursues its course, food becomes chyle and blood.

Thus, to maintain living bodies is of more concrete, vital interest than to keep a fine floor in proper condition; the cook's effort is evidently transcended toward the future. If, however, it is better to share in another's free transcendence than to lose oneself in things, it is not less dangerous. The validity of the cook's work is to be found only in the mouths of those around her table; she needs their approbation, demands that they appreciate her dishes and call for second helpings; she is upset if they are not hungry, to the point that one wonders whether the fried potatoes are for her husband or her husband for the fried potatoes. This ambiguity is evident in the general attitude of the housekeeping wife: she takes care of the house for her husband; but she also wants him to spend all he earns for furnishings and an electric refrigerator. She desires to make him happy; but she approves of his activities only in so far as they fall within the frame of happiness she has set up.

There have been times when these claims have in general found satisfaction: times when such felicity was also man's ideal, when he was attached above all to his home, to his family, and when even the children chose to be characterized by their parents, their traditions, and their past. At such times she who ruled the home, who presided at the dinner table, was recognized as supreme; and she still plays this

linen is scorched, the roast burns, chinaware gets broken; these are absolute disasters, for when things are destroyed, they are gone forever. Permanence and security cannot possibly be obtained through them. The pillage and bombs of war threaten one's wardrobes, one's house.

The products of domestic work, then, must necessarily be consumed; a continual renunciation is required of the woman whose operations are completed only in their destruction. For her to acquiesce without regret, these minor holocausts must at least be reflected in someone's joy or pleasure. But since the housekeeper's labor is expended to maintain the *status quo*, the husband, coming into the house, may notice disorder or negligence, but it seems to him that order and neatness come of their own accord. He has a more positive interest in a good meal. The cook's moment of triumph arrives when she puts a successful dish on the table: husband and children receive it with warm approval, not only in words, but by consuming it gleefully. The culinary alchemy then pursues its course, food becomes chyle and blood.

Thus, to maintain living bodies is of more concrete, vital interest than to keep a fine floor in proper condition; the cook's effort is evidently transcended toward the future. If, however, it is better to share in another's free transcendence than to lose oneself in things, it is not less dangerous. The validity of the cook's work is to be found only in the mouths of those around her table; she needs their approbation, demands that they appreciate her dishes and call for second helpings; she is upset if they are not hungry, to the point that one wonders whether the fried potatoes are for her husband or her husband for the fried potatoes. This ambiguity is evident in the general attitude of the housekeeping wife: she takes care of the house for her husband; but she also wants him to spend all he earns for furnishings and an electric refrigerator. She desires to make him happy; but she approves of his activities only in so far as they fall within the frame of happiness she has set up.

There have been times when these claims have in general found satisfaction: times when such felicity was also man's ideal, when he was attached above all to his home, to his family, and when even the children chose to be characterized by their parents, their traditions, and their past. At such times she who ruled the home, who presided at the dinner table, was recognized as supreme; and she still plays this

▶ Setting Up the Page As she worked on the last spread, Murray found that the highlighted words "seemed to pop off the page, they were so appropriate." Here, she has painted the page blue, leaving the chosen words unpainted and adding some blocks of pale peach. At this early stage, one can see how she has set up several small canvases she can later fill with images and patterns.

▶ Integrating Elements Taking her color cue from the peach, the artist stamped an image of a woman reading a book in dark coral, using a makeup sponge to apply the paint. The dots at top left are contact-paper scraps from another project. A dark edge of paint stamped with pale lines helps frame the page. To visually integrate the blocks, she applied a self-carved stamp using terracotta paint.

▼ Final Details Here, further layers have been added, using paint applied with stamps and brushes. She chose lighter and darker values of the same colors and one or two contrasting colors, often applying more than one color to the same stamp. Using a fine brush, she added crisp lines and edges, then incorporated handwriting to personalize the page. Finally, she linked and framed the words: "the filled pages say all. IL FINE."

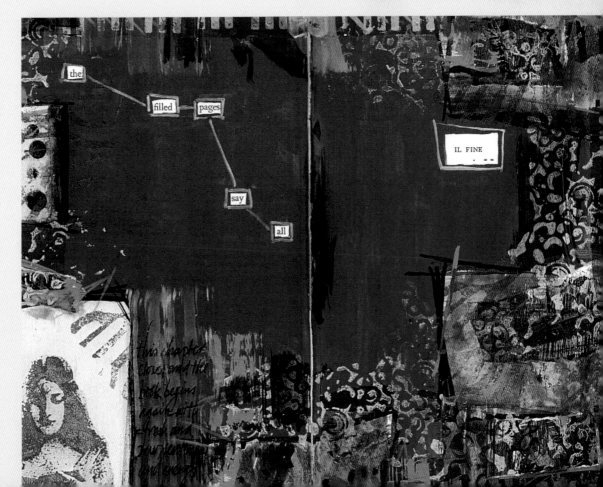

A popular book-altering technique is cutting a window to reveal part of another page, and here Melissa McCobb Hubbell uses it to great effect. With careful forethought (it can be tricky getting the placement right), she cut windows through several pages, then

The Rose

Melissa McCobb Hubbell

bookended them with portraits placed so only the eyes would be visible. She worked the pages, painting them with washes of acrylic, adding collage elements, and burning the window edges to soften the cut line. The result: A mysterious, romantic set of pages that gradually reveals the enigmatic, dark-eyed woman who inhabits the book.

MATERIALS found papers or images • acrylic paints • printing ink or inkpads • brayer • assorted rubber stamps • acrylic matte medium (used as an adhesive) • matches, dish of water (for burning technique, see page 33) • basic supplies (see page 9)

▶ **Using Found Materials** On the first page of *The Rose*, dark eyes peer through an opening in the flowers, as if the woman portrayed is wearing a veil of roses. The project makes clever use of found paper—the large tissue paper roses are cheese tray decorations and were purchased at a gourmet shop. Tiny ladybug stickers complete the picture, their shininess reduced with a dab of acrylic matte medium.

◄ Altering an Image Here, McCobb Hubbell used a pre-existing image in the book (a large watercolor illustration of a red rose) as her base, darkening and intensifying it with acrylic paints. Burning softened the window edges, creating an impression of kohl-smudged eyes. She collaged on insect stickers and text cut from a previous page, and distressed the whole page using black ink and a rubber brayer.

◄ Applying Ink with a Brayer The large crucifix that dominates this altered page (the back of the preceding page shown above) was added using black printing ink and a rubber brayer. To create the effect, spread a dollop of printing ink on a sheet of glass. Dip a brayer in the ink and roll it back and forth until it is evenly coated. For a mottled effect, roll the brayer across scrap paper first to remove some of the ink. (Another method is to substitute an inkpad for printing ink.) The patterns and images were made using stamps.

► On the following page, the artist has scanned the image of a woman's face and, using Photoshop, manipulated the colors and saturation, adding a layer of turquoise blue. She then printed the image onto cotton rag paper and adhered it to the book with acrylic matte medium. Layers of aqua pastel, gold acrylic, and stamps lend texture and detail to the printout.

...anting of rose... g... a rose garden to be ...anted to provide fresh roses to strew over his grave. ...s heirs would meet on the anniversary of his death ...crown his tomb with roses from the garden.

The custom survived for many centuries, for as late ...1653 a citizen of London, Edward Rose, left a legacy ...£20 to purchase an acre of land in Barnes, Surrey, ...r the use of the poor. The conditions were that he ...ould be buried there, and that the roses he ordered ...be planted ...

...When Vic... ...membering t... ...es were in bl... ...friend of the... ...arden so that, ...the grave to... ...In Turkey... ...married wo... ...anting roses... ...ries were kno...

CHARM...

...he rose buds...

...AKE three... ...t to the heat... ...days more... ...to the one... ...ved...

...ove... ...ion... ...d red from... ...tcheraft... ...day and... ...rose per... ...mmer's... ...usband, wo... ...ood and kep... ...enuty in a dr... ...se would be... ...d stored away... ...refully.

many a rose was never thrown into an open tomb, for he who threw it would supposedly wither and die by some form of magic.

A red rose from which the petals fell while it was being carried or worn has in many countries been regarded as an omen of death. In much of the Christian world the red rose is a symbol of evil, perhaps because of an old belief that the crown of thorns which Jesus wore was made of rose briars, and from the blood ... thorns ...

If it had withered, the lover had been untrue; but if it ll showed traces of its midsummer colour, the lover s faithful. Following the principle that for every ill

advocated the use of rose hips to supply this vital vitamin for babies and young children, for the gardens an hedgerows of Britain abound in the rich red hips

Technique Highlight:
DIGITAL ART

Even for artists who don't wish to create purely digital art, graphics software can be a wonderful tool that adds further dimension and possibility to mixed-media collage and altered books.

When working in Adobe Photoshop, scan your own artwork—drawings, paintings, mixed-media collages, or altered book pages. This will allow you to then rework your original piece, resizing, changing the hue, adding layers, inverting to a negative, or creating repeats or variations. Some useful techniques:

• Use Photoshop's layer effects to alter the coloration or texture of your image.

• Invert an image to a negative of the original. Printed on vellum or acetate, this creates a transparency and adds interest when used as an overlay.

• Flip the image and create a mirror version of your original work.

• Add line art or text in a Photoshop layer to create further dimension in the original work.

• Select and copy areas of the original and make repeat patterns. Repeating your primary image in various sizes, colors, or effects can strengthen a themed piece.

Graphics programs are also useful for altering a found image or text to better fit the format of your book page:

• Scan a copyright-free image and adjust the size or proportion to fit.

• Desaturate a color image to create a black-and-white picture.

• Add a color layer to tint the image. Sepia brown will create a vintage look.

• Layer several images for a transfer or collaged look.

• Edit areas of the original image that don't fit with the piece.

• Add text.

The best thing to do is to experiment with digital graphics software and see how you can make it work for you. By scanning found images and your own original work, you can create a library of signature images you will use again and again.

—Melissa McCobb Hubbell

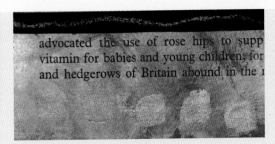

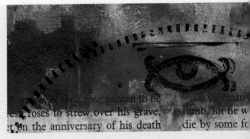

Melissa McCobb Hubbell on digital art

"It's important to look at your art in a different way. It's so hard to be objective about your own work. One of the things I love about digital art is that you can quickly invert your art to a negative or completely change the colors, or you can crop it or flip it horizontally and see it in a new way."

a birdlike heart

LK Ludwig

LK Ludwig used a vintage German music book to chronicle the months preceding the birth of her daughter and her divorce. The title—a birdlike heart—refers to the quickness of a bird's heartbeat, referencing both the rapid heart rate of her unborn child and the anxious nature of this time in her life. Here, the page has been covered with shiny duct tape, which was sanded and smeared with paint, offering an intriguing contrast to natural elements such as feathers, garnets, and sheets of silvery mica tacked over a photo transfer of the artist's newborn daughter.

MATERIALS texts such as bird definition and a printout on tea-dyed paper • embellishments such as bird feathers, beads, claw, mica • Chartpak blender (for photo transfer) • black acrylic paint • HVAC duct tape and copper tape • metal tab, paper fasteners, and wire • sanding block • basic supplies (see page 9)

LK Ludwig on her favorite techniques

"I use a lot of my own photography, whether it's transfers or transparencies or actual photographs, in collages. I work a little bit with metal, and I use paint. I would recommend that people buy *The Artist's Manual* or a book that describes different media, so that if you have an idea in your head, you can find out if you can do it. Some things can be layered, others can't; some things will retain their vibrancy, others won't. That way you'll know what your various supplies are capable of doing."

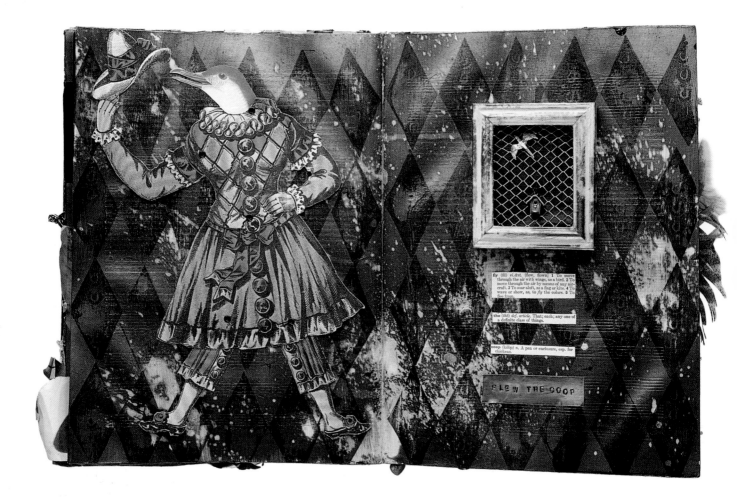

▲ Adding Metal to Books To build a sturdy work surface, the artist glued pages together in groups of four. The background is copper paint (containing actual copper flakes), patinaed and stamped with a diamond shape. Metallic paints can bring an unexpected quality to books, creating the illusion of metal and forming a rich backdrop for interesting add-ons such as copper mesh, silver charms, tags, eyelets, vintage toys, and more.

▶ Photo Transfers, Drawing, and Collage
A photo-transferred image of the artist appears to float above the page; the musical score is visible through the figure, providing a reference to bird-song. The image was further worked with black pencil and charcoal, and adorned with colorful birds and text clipped from vintage birding books.

In using photo transfers, the original artwork is preserved, and the transfer process softens the image, often producing a watercolor effect. Generally speaking, photo transfers fall into two categories: those involving toner copies (photocopies or laser printouts) and those involving inkjet printouts. Both types work with black-and-white or color originals.

Technique Highlight:
PHOTO TRANSFERS

Toner copy transfers are released using a solvent, such as acetone (black-and-white only), xylene, Citrasolve, oil of wintergreen, or paint thinner. Always work in a well-ventilated area, far from an open flame, wearing rubber gloves. Inkjet transfers can be done using water or acrylic gel medium, though neither process works well with archival inks. (Note: For text or an image where direction matters, flip it before printing. To reverse a photocopy, copy the image onto a transparency, flip it over, and recopy.)

- **For toner copy transfers:** Place the image face down on the transfer surface. Apply solvent to the back with a clean white rag. Burnish with a bone folder or wooden spoon.

- **For a one-step transfer:** Chartpak colorless blenders are markers filled with xylene. The application of solvent and burnishing are all in one step. This makes them very handy for small images and working directly on a book page. See pages 25 and 26 for examples.

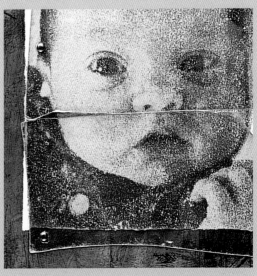

- **For water transfers:** Print an image onto glossy ink-jet photo paper, spray the transfer surface with water, apply the photo paper image side down, and burnish. The amount of water depends on the texture and rag content of the transfer surface: Slick paper requires less water and textured more.

- **For gel medium transfers:** Print your image onto cheap (not quick-dry) inkjet transparencies, generously apply gel medium to the transfer surface, apply the image, and burnish.

- **For an easy, solvent-free transfer:** Place clear packing tape on an image (a magazine page, laser print or color photocopy) and press down. Soak in water, then remove paper residue with your fingertips; the ink will remain on the tape. Glue the tape to your book page or over a cutout to create a stunning window. This technique also works with clear shelf-lining paper, which comes in a matte finish and can accommodate large images.

—LK Ludwig

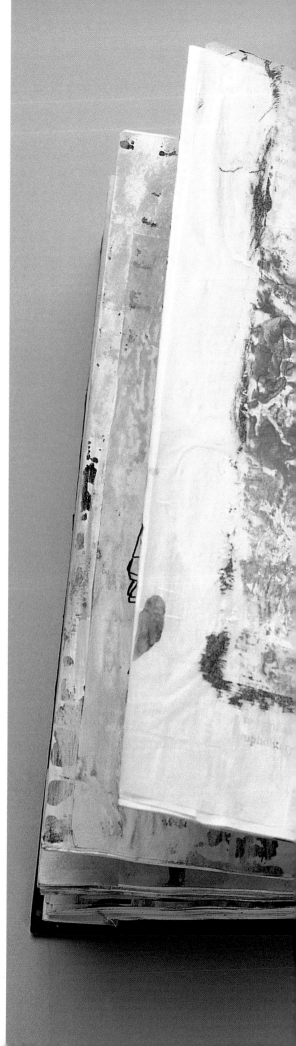

VIV

Altering books came naturally to Deborah Putnoi, a collage artist with an affinity for using her own and found texts. She turned a novel into an art journal by pasting together several pages and wrapping them with tracing paper. She then covered the soft, thick pages in layers of paint, pressing them together and pulling them apart to create random textures and adding sinewy line drawings. The translucent nature of the paper and paint allow the book's original text to assert itself in places, creating a dialogue between the author's words and the artist's imagery.

Deborah Putnoi

MATERIALS collage elements • tempera paint • tracing paper • ink • acrylic gel medium • PVA glue • basic supplies (see page 9)

▼ **Creating a Series** The intimate nature of the book format is enhanced by the directness and immediacy of Putnoi's style. Here, an inky figure stares out of the pages, surrounded by a field of orange flecked with green and white. Conceived as a series, the other pages feature the same painterly approach along with landscape elements, drawings of deer, and partial images of hands. As you work on your own book, keep in mind that you don't have to rely on words to tell a story.

Deborah Putnoi on choosing a book "The size and shape of a book grab me initially. I alter books containing images and text; each offers different experiences and problems to solve. Using a text-based book, I like to pick out random words and use them in the collage. Images are more difficult, but the results are often exciting and bizarre."

ABC Board Book

▲ **Subtracting and Adding Images** The artist used a small-format children's board book as a springboard for exploring a fragment of the alphabet. She dedicated each page to a different letter by painting over the text until just one letter remained. She also subtracted imagery, leaving baby faces and hands visible, before adding fabric and paper collage elements, patterns and lines of color, and scratching out images and words in the paint. The result is a colorful and playful book that begs to have its pages turned.

- **Cut.** Cut windows to emphasize special imagery.

- **Highlight.** Highlight words to build a narrative; highlight images to make a visual story.

- **Attach.** Attach glassine envelopes and tuck in mini collages or tag art; attach handmade-paper envelopes and include personal messages, poems, or stories.

Some Fun Things to Do to Books

Whatever your usual media, you can bring your skills to the making of artist books, journals, and altered books. To get you started, here's a list of things to try:

- **Carve.** Carve a niche and fill it with resin or add geological specimens, small figurines, a mirror.

- **Glue.** Glue pages together to thicken them; glue tissue over pages to veil the text.

- **Rip and tear.** Rip pages to alter the edges; tear up extras for collaging.

- **Sew.** Sew on flaps to hide and reveal images; sew pages together with a zigzag stitch and metallic thread; sew on buttons, fabric scraps, rickrack, ribbon.

- **Punch.** Punch in grommets and use wire to attach trinkets, metal scraps, stones; punch out holes with craft punches: stars, circles, triangles, moons.

- **Paint.** Paint a page lightly and let the text show through; paint lots of layers and obscure it.

- **Insert.** Insert translucent materials between two window cutouts: mica, photocopies on acetate, colorful vellums.

- **Transfer.** Transfer photocopied images onto painted or collaged pages.

- **Sand and abrade.** Sand painted pages to reveal hidden images or text; abrade the cover to age it.

- **Collage.** Collage found papers, decorative papers, fabric, or metal foils onto the pages.

- **Stamp.** Stamp images and designs; stamp words to add found poems, personal messages, comment on a theme.

- **Drill.** Drill into the cover and lace through colorful ribbons and yarns.

- **Ink.** Ink random patterns on a page or cover; ink a page with sepia or deep blue to add nostalgia, darkness, mystery.

- **Saw.** Saw a book into a unique shape: a semi-circle, house, hand, mask, or fish.

- **Layer.** Layer pages so they interact over four or five spreads, with half-pages, transparencies, and window cutouts.

To learn new techniques, join a round robin or an online discussion group, subscribe to a zine, or talk to your friends. Helga Strauss features new techniques in an illustrated quarterly column in *ARTitude Zine*. (See page 125 for Web site.) The burning technique is from the Winter 2001 issue.

BURNING

Burning adds soft lines and a sense of mystery. To burn the edges of a page or window, dip a brush in water and draw a wiggly line just past your planned burn line. This ensures the whole page won't catch on fire. Lift the page and light it. Keep a damp cloth handy, in case the firewall fails. (Note: A candle can be used to age a book without burning. Set the smoke marks with a fixative spray.)

The Optimist's Good Nigh

Sharon McCartney's altered book transforms a vintage volume containing daily meditations on life by nineteenth-century writers. Using the original text as her point of departure, she created artwork and a new text focusing on life cycles and survival. Her text

What Survives)

Sharon McCartney

is a found poem, made by isolating words and covering the rest of the page with gesso. The lines are scattered over pages delicately embellished with painted and drawn images, gelatin prints, photo transfers, hand sewing, and collage. The book contains several flaps, woven pages, and an unusual zoological shrine.

MATERIALS hand-printed and vintage papers • found text, such as old botany and zoology books • natural elements, such as fossilized sand dollars • watercolor and acrylic paints • gesso • pastels • tea bag • metallic thread • PVA glue • basic supplies (see page 9)

▶ **Creating a Shrine** Turning the pages of the book finally reveals a cutout that enshrines two fossilized sand dollars. To fashion it, the artist cut a deep niche, then wrapped the block of cut pages with soft rice paper before adhering it inside the back cover. A niche provides an opportunity to showcase interesting found objects. Consider items that embody or comment upon the theme of your book or even ones that subvert the narrative.

Pond

▶ Affecting a Book's Flow

The following three photographs show pages from McCartney's mixed-media nature journal, *Pond*. Here, she has treated the spread as a single canvas, painting both sides green and letting images of water plants, frogs, and amoeba-like organisms transverse the join. To alter a book's flow, treat the individual pages as canvases with an occasional united spread serving as a visual point of rest. Alternately, move the viewer through the book more slowly, spread to spread.

▼ Sewing and Stitching

Demonstrating how sewing can be used for more than binding pages together, this spread features a flap that lifts to reveal a painted mushroom. Instead of gluing the flap in place, the artist sewed the bottom half to the page, framing the painting with a line of slanted stitches. The effect is echoed with another line of stitching around the edges of the lifted top. Even such subtle repetitions and details add a compelling element to the composition of a page.

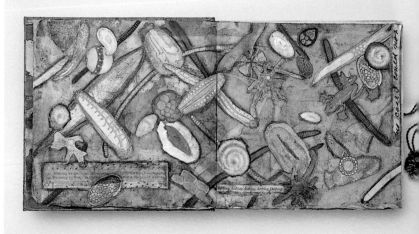

Within the collage image, the following text appears:

> This rather attractive but common plant is the Self-heal or Heal-all, naturalized from Europe and Asia, but is also a native of this country. It is found from New-foundland to Flor-ida and on west across the continent. It grows in old fields and out of the way places. It belongs to the Mint Family but does not

> SELF-HEAL OR HEAL-ALL

> dream of   you   when fast   a - sleep,
> brings to   us   the morn-ing   dew.

▲ Working with Original and Found Art This colorful page is a prime example of how McCartney works, by intermingling her own artwork with sampled texts and printed images. "I love the texture and softness of old paper," she says, "and find it soaks up paint differently than the highly sized newer papers, leaving a more muted and saturated color." Notice how the found and artist-generated images blend easily to create a harmonious whole. Consider this when choosing collage materials: Found imagery can augment your style or act as a visual foil to add contrast or drama.

| **Sharon McCartney on artist books** | "I use the book to create an intimacy with the viewer that is harder to achieve with larger painted works. Viewing a book—holding it in your hand, turning its pages—is a very intentional, private act. One is able to possess this piece of art for a moment. I like books that feel good to the hand, are small enough to encourage intimacy, and have a weather-beaten feel that suggests a history and discovery of a treasure from the past." |

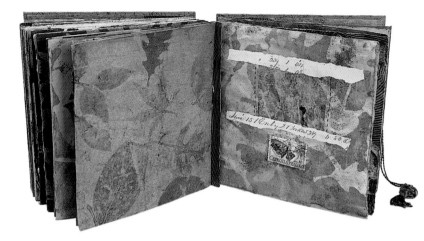

◄ Adding Drama with Natural Materials
When working with natural materials, consider the best way to show off their special qualities. Here, the artist has created a window that has a "pane"—actually translucent mica sandwiched between two pages and exposed by cutout squares. Keeping the rest of the page simple (it's embellished only with soft gelatin prints, see page 39 for the technique), she accentuates the mica's fragile beauty.

Finds

▼ Suspending Images in Windows This spread is from McCartney's altered antique photo album, *Finds*, in which the images are built around the window structure of each page. Here, a watercolor painting of an egg is suspended in the window by black threads; this dynamic approach draws attention to the egg while providing glimpses of the following page as part of the egg's visual context. A different approach could be to substitute metal wire for the thread; it comes in many colors and can be twisted into curlicues and other shapes.

This simple monoprinting process uses a sheet of gelatin as its "plate." After inking, you can create impressions with textured objects or by drawing gently on the surface using any rounded instrument. The gelatin is quite sensitive and will pick up very subtle patterns and textures.

Technique Highlight:

GELATIN PRINTS

1. Mix gelatin according to the "gelatin squares" recipe on box, substituting water for juice. Pour into pan until $1/2$" (1 cm) deep, and use a spoon to pull air bubbles to the sides. Let stand until it sets, then refrigerate. Do not cover or touch the surface prior to printing. The plate should last three days, longer if refrigerated. (Note: Work up two at a time, in case one cracks.)

2. On the glass palette, ink a brayer, then roll a thin layer of ink onto the plate. Roll a few layers to deepen color, or lay different colors on top of one another. Once the plate is inked, work quickly. (Spray with water if needed to revive inks.)

3. Use tweezers to gently lay mark-making objects on plate and smooth down with fingers. Lifting objects before printing will impart subtle and detailed impressions, and leaving them on when you print will create silhouette images. To achieve multiple layers of images and color, ink stamps and objects and lightly press them onto plate. When using lace or fabric, press down with newsprint to remove excess ink and make even impressions.

4. Lay paper over the prepared plate and gently burnish with fingers or the back of a spoon. Peel off and set aside to dry. You can get both a positive and negative print out of the same plate by adding then removing objects and building up layers of images. Clean the plate with a sponge and water between prints.

—Sharon McCartney

MATERIALS unflavored gelatin • 13" x 9" (33 cm x 23 cm) low-sided metal pan (do not reuse for food) • smooth, lightweight paper (such as rice paper) • water-soluble printing inks or watercolor paints in tubes • palette made of glass or Plexiglas • brayers • textured objects such as lace, leaves, mesh, bubble wrap, stamps (avoid things that shed or have sharp protrusions) • sponge and water • spray bottle • tweezers • newsprint • basic supplies (see page 9)

A popular form of collaborating among altered book artists is to participate in a round robin, where artists alter spreads in each other's books. Here's how it works: Once the players are set (either by signing up through an Internet site or getting friends together), each player starts a book, establishing a theme and sometimes a color scheme. Each month, the players receive a new book and send the one they've worked in to the next person in the queue. When the books have gone full circle, each one will contain artwork by all of the players.

Collaborations

The spreads shown in this chapter are from a volume that was part of a seven-book round robin started by Helga Strauss. "I decided to organize the *Artarama* round robin because I wanted to pull together a group of artists that I greatly admire," she says. "Each of their styles is unique and expressive." They were all artists she knew through *ARTitude Zine*, art retreats, and swaps, and this was a chance to get to know them better and share an artistic experience. With seven players, it took about nine months to complete the project.

The pages featured are from Sarah Fishburn's book—actually an old record album holder found at a yard sale. Structured like a book, with sleeves for 45s in place of pages, it was stuffed with old records. To establish a theme connected to her mother, Fishburn called the project *What My Mother Played*, referencing child's play and playing music. She left the 45s in the sleeves intending them as gifts for the others. Not surprisingly, some of the players ended up altering the records along with the pages.

Artist: Suz Simanaitis

Artist: Helga Strauss

Books by their very nature are interactive, and in a successful round robin players will embrace this in numerous ways, such as hiding art or messages inside envelopes or tucking gifts for the other players into the pages. In *What My Mother Played*, Strauss slipped vintage ephemera into a record sleeve then decorated the outside with art made out of a picture and an aluminum light reflector (above left). She wrote a little note around the flower to draw Fishburn's attention to the gifts inside.

Although people's reasons for joining a round robin will likely vary—maybe the theme is appealing, or the type of book is fun, or the other artists are the draw—one thing they will have in common is the shared experience of working in the same books. The collaborative process offers artists a chance to learn new techniques from each other, to be inspired by different approaches, and to adapt those ideas to fit their own artistic style.

KEEP A COPY

Because your art won't be accessible once it moves on, you might want to document it by making color photocopies, pictures, slides, or scans. Many artists scan their work and post images on their Web sites. If you are hoping to publish your work, make slides or hi-resolution scans and keep a record of who has it, just in case you need to borrow it.

"She Had No Paper for Drawing"

Sarah Fishburn

Sarah Fishburn on making altered books

"As an artist, what's important is to express what's inside of you. Don't worry about it being good enough; just do what your heart tells you. Play and don't get stressed out. Altered books are a fun medium; there's so much potential with them, and everyone has something unique to offer. Plus, it's really pleasurable to sit on the couch with a friend, looking at everything, just turning pages of a book."

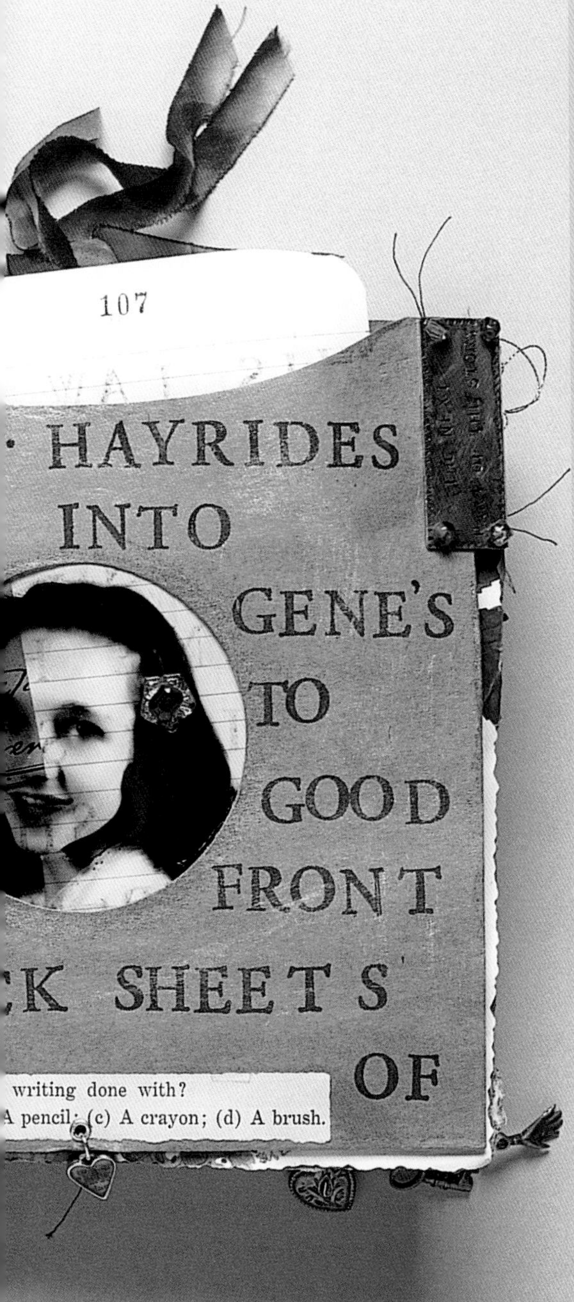

107

· HAYRIDES
INTO
GENE'S
TO
GOOD
FRONT
K SHEETS
OF

writing done with?
A pencil; (c) A crayon; (d) A brush.

To connect her wish to commemorate her mother and the unique structure of the record album "book," Sarah Fishburn gave it the theme and title of What My Mother Played, *referencing child's play as well as playing music. Pictured here is the sign-on page with signatures of the artists and the titles of their pages. On the opposite page, the first in the book, Sarah has imagined her mother's life growing up in the 1930s and 1940s. In the center is a photograph of her mother she made luminous by printing it on acetate. A chalk background stamped with words representing her mother's thoughts surrounds it, along with such collage elements as a charm made by a friend and a quote from a vintage child's primer. Tucked into the sleeve is a surprise: a tag ornamented with ribbons, fibers, and beads.*

MATERIALS paper ephemera such as found text and photographs • embellishments such as ribbons, fibers, beads, faux jewels, charms • rubberstamp alphabet and black dye ink • colored chalk • acetate • cardstock • acid-free glue stick • basic supplies (see page 9)

"Summer, 1948"
and "The Little Musicians"

Suz Simanaitis

She lived in the city, but for one bright afternoon in 1948 she was the Sweetheart of the Rodeo...

"One thing I find ironic is that a lot of people are frantic to 'learn the rules' or special techniques, when, to my way of thinking, the rule is that there are no rules and no techniques that can't be tried. Altered books can incorporate unusual bindings, niches, drawers and doors, pop-up elements, stitchery, things that spin. There really is nothing one couldn't try."

Suz Simanaitis addressed the round robin theme by splitting it, devoting half the spread to her mother and the other half to the idea of play. On the left, she started with a photograph of her mom as a little girl, seated on a pony and looking like she hasn't a care in the world. To preserve the original, she used a photocopy, embellishing the chaps with star-shaped confetti. A background of painted tissue paper hides the sleeve hole, varying the composition, and computer-generated text provides a whimsical narrative. On the right, she created a lively collage using Japanese paper, cheap cocktail napkins, and photocopies of Cicely Mary Barker fairies. She also altered one of the records (see photograph, page 40). Be open to the possibilities offered by your book: If there's a pocket, put something surprising inside it—an altered photograph, a mini collage, or even a tiny altered book.

MATERIALS black-and-white and color photocopies • paper ephemera such as Japanese *washi*, cocktail napkins, confetti • found text • acrylic paints and gold powdered pigment • inkpads • for record album: wallpaper scraps, photocopies of vintage postcards, glitter glue, ribbon • PVA glue • basic supplies (see page 9)

Artarama: What My Mother Played

"Little Red Riding Hood" and "Little Seamstress"

Jill S. Haddaway

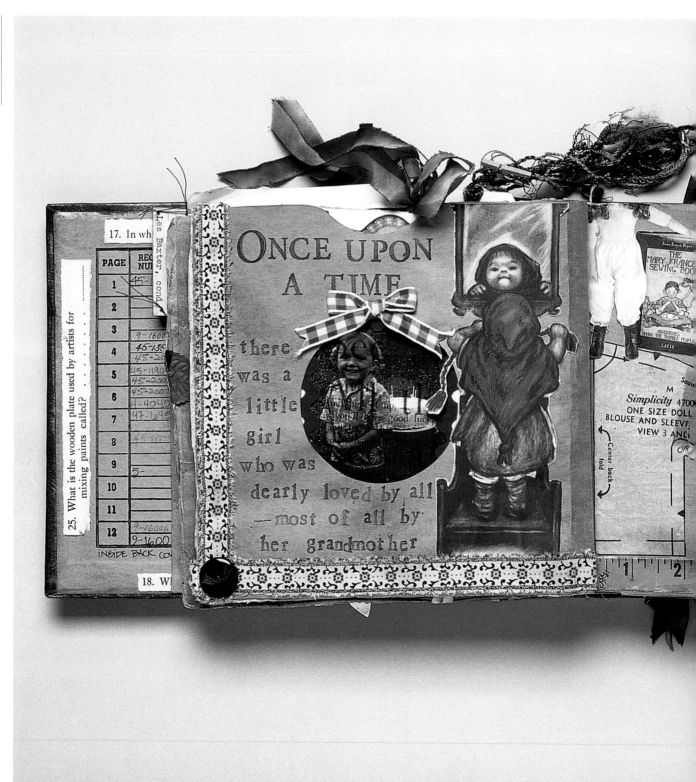

"I can't praise the round robin experience highly enough. There is no better way to grow as an altered book artist than to see these works firsthand. Every time a book arrives in the mailbox, it's a tingly moment: You carefully turn each page and cry, 'You can do that?' or 'I've got to try that!' "

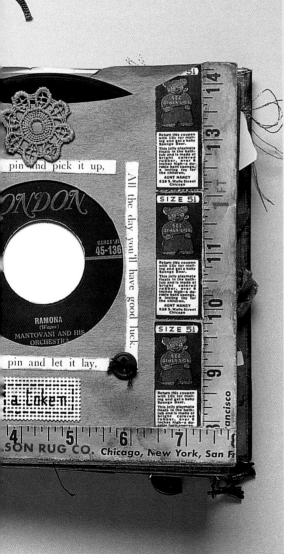

In this collage spread, Jill Haddaway addresses the theme by honoring her mother. First she set a nostalgic tone by aging the record sleeves with sandalwood ink, a demonstration of how easily color can be used to establish a mood. "Little Red Riding Hood" was created using found objects, paper ephemera, and book illustrations depicting the fairytale heroine, a family favorite, peering at herself in the mirror. The little face peeking out of the center is the artist's mother as a child. For "Little Seamstress," Haddaway used doll-pattern pieces, measuring tape, and other sewing notions to commemorate her mother's skill as a seamstress. Memorabilia can provide a simple yet effective link to your subject. When commemorating a person, search out items that reflect something personal about him or her: handwriting samples, photographs at different ages, or objects that represent a favorite activity—fishing lures, foreign stamps, theater tickets.

MATERIALS sewing notions such as buttons, embroidery floss, ribbon, measuring tape • paper ephemera such as doll pattern pieces, book illustrations, text • tiny tea-stained doily • decorative needle case covers • perforated paper with cross-stitched motto • sandalwood ink • acrylic matte medium • basic supplies (see page 9)

"Let's Play Dress Up" and "Come Fly with Me"

Karenann Young

Karenann Young on collaborative creativity

"Working in an altered-book round robin was a huge growth experience for me. I learned a lot from everyone's work. It was a challenge working in different books with various themes, and it really helped me stretch my creativity in ways that I normally wouldn't have tried."

Karenann Young turned her pages into playful dress-up fantasies. For "Let's Play Dress-Up," she used rubber stamps to make collage materials for the background and directly on the surface. A tinted black-and-white image of a young girl wearing a flounced dress and flowered hat establishes a nostalgic mood; she is surrounded by lavishly costumed ladies, who preen and pose with happy abandon. Even the page itself is dressed up in gathered lace and a shiny jewel. "Come Fly with Me" features a winged diva inviting us to join her on a musical adventure. Fanciful collage elements such as gold wings and a doily heighten the whimsical mood. When working on your own book, consider how pattern pieces, fabrics, and sewing notions can express other themes related to the female form and styles of dress.

MATERIALS collage elements such as lace, jewels, computer-generated text • black-and-white and color images from old books • gold doily and fabric wings • acrylic paints • acrylic gel medium • rubber stamps • basic supplies (see page 9)

"Marseillaise" and
"She Wanted to Go to Paris"

Kristin Ashton

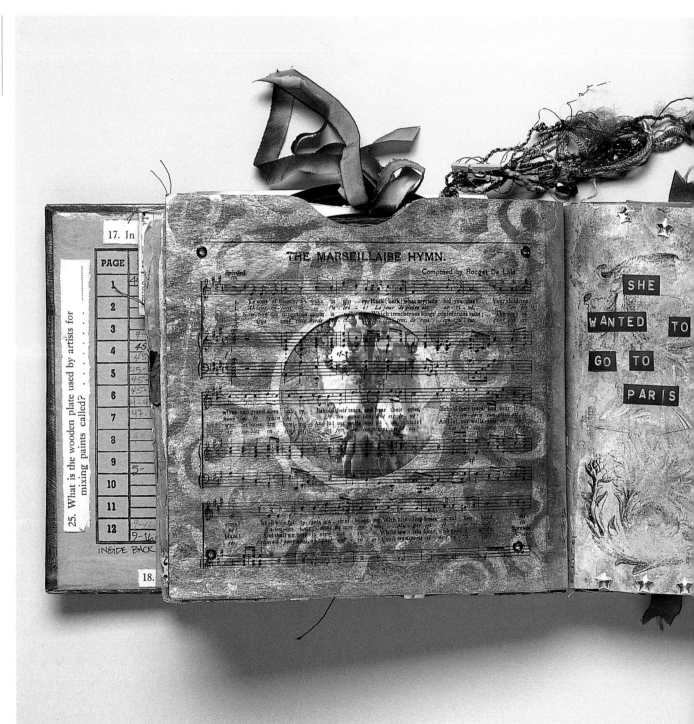

"I found the way the books evolved and took on a life of their own to be magical. I anticipated each book's arrival like it was Christmas Day. The artwork was so inspiring and unique. I have created lifelong friends in this exchange, in addition to learning many wonderful new techniques and perspectives in art, collage, and altered books."

A collage artist, Kristin Ashton had never done an altered book before joining the Artarama round robin. She used her skills to wash the surface with pink and purple acrylics, adding stamped swirls as well as transparent and opaque collage elements to create a multi-layered effect. She then photocopied the "Marseillaise" hymn onto acetate and floated it over the colorful background, attaching it with grommets. A tiny collage tucked into the record sleeve is partially visible through the round opening. "She Wanted to Go to Paris" is ornamented with photo transfers of clip art. Ashton took advantage of the built-in peek-a-boo central opening, backing it with a Moulin Rouge postcard and layering an acetate photocopy of an actress on top. When altering books or booklike objects, let the structural elements inspire creative approaches: Create a shrine in a recess, use flaps to hide images, or cut down a large book into an interesting shape.

MATERIALS found papers such as sheet music, vintage postcards, colorful ephemera • art papers such as hot-press watercolor paper, cardstock • transparency film (for inkjet printers) • black-and-white photocopies of clip art • acrylic paints • label maker and black tape • star scrapbook punch • foam stamp and metallic inkpad • grommets • craft jewels • acid-free glue stick • acrylic matte medium • clear caulk • basic supplies (see page 9)

MAKING PHOTO TRANSFERS USING CAULK AS A SOLVENT

Apply clear caulk to a black-and-white photocopy. Place photocopy face down on the page, smoothing away air bubbles. When the caulk is dry, rub away the paper residue with washcloth and water. See page 27 for other photo transfer techniques.

"She Plays"

Helga Strauss

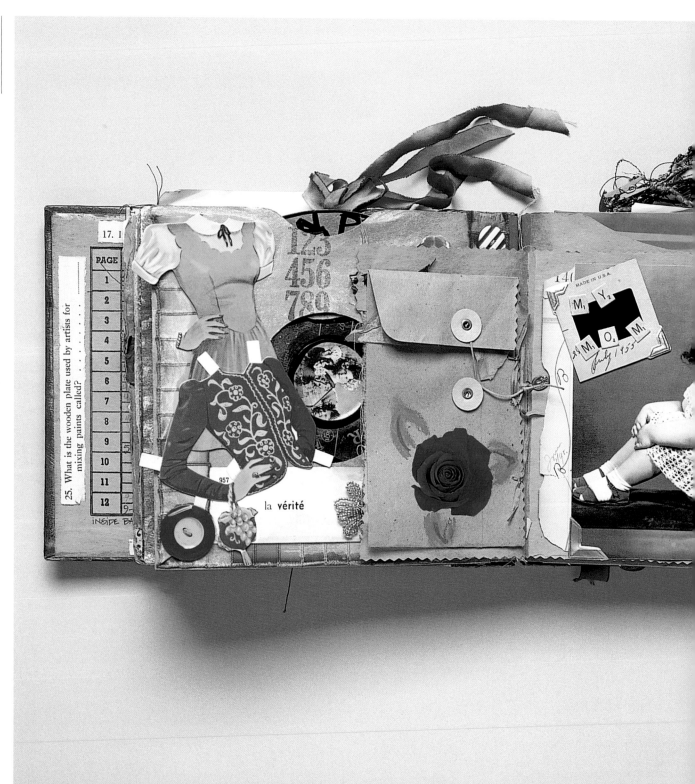

Helga Strauss on discovering altered books

Helga Strauss on discovering altered books

"Somebody in one of the Yahoo groups started talking about working in old books. I collect old books and have always done collage. So the first time I did it, I instantly knew, 'This is for me.' Combining my two loves—books and collage—what could be better? I've also dabbled in different media like oil painting and jewelry making, and with altered books you can bring all of your skills into one place."

As a young girl, her mother sewed fashionable out-fits for all of her dolls, so Helga Strauss chose sewing notions to honor this early pastime. To make the page interactive, she added "doors" by cutting a line through the center of the top of the record sleeve and along the edges, and then folding each half back. The outside is covered with fabric, buttons, and vintage tinsel and has a hook closure. Inside, she added a photo of her mom as a child and adhered an envelope containing a special message. She completed the interior with rose stickers, drawn leaves, an old slide, and photocopies of Scrabble tiles.

MATERIALS paper ephemera such as photographs, envelopes, stickers • sewing notions • water-soluble oil pastels • old slide • vintage tinsel • acid-free glue stick • basic supplies (see page 9)

One of the unique things about altered books is that they are an interactive art form. You can emphasize this by providing flaps to lift, strings or ribbons to untie, scrolls to unfurl, and envelopes and boxes to peek into.

Artarama: What My Mother Played

"Parrucche 1800–1900"
and "Très Groovy"

Cathleen Perkins

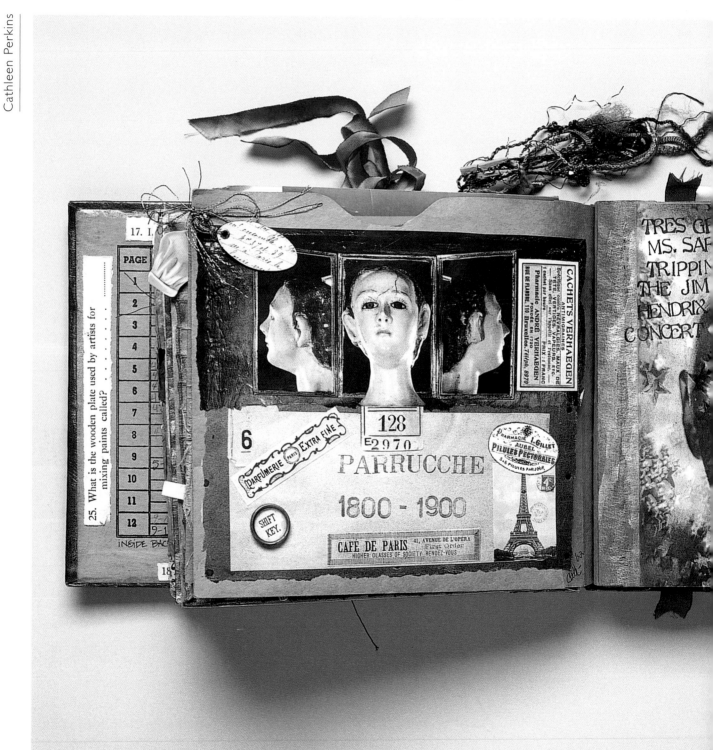

"When I received my own book back, I realized what a true treasure I had participated in. The pages were beautiful and filled with so many wonderful artful ways of relating to my theme. I learned so much about new ways to plan pages that I'd never thought of before."

Working intuitively, Cathleen Perkins collaged the left side of the spread with paper ephemera and found objects according to a French theme. Uniting the spread through the color palette, she used the right side for a completely different theme: to celebrate the grooviness of the 1960s and 1970s in honor of Sarah Fishburn, who loves the era. The artist altered her "groovy gal" using metallic paints and stars and applied a personal message with alphabet stamps and her friend's nickname with Scrabble letters.

Focusing on a specific time period can provide a lively subject for a round robin, with a rich world of pop culture imagery available in vintage books, fashion or lifestyle magazines, calendars, and other printed matter. Mix it up and place yourself or pictures of people you know into period outfits or foreign settings.

MATERIALS paper images, including photograph of a groovy gal • found objects such as vintage typewriter keys, game pieces, old French pharmacy labels • metallic paints • metal eyelets and tag • metallic thread • alphabet rubber stamps and inkpad • acid-free glue stick and PVA glue • basic supplies (see page 9)

An ongoing project of mass proportions, the 1,000 Journals Project is a sort of mega-round robin started in August 2000 by a San Francisco graphic artist who calls himself "someguy."

PROJECT HIGHLIGHT: 1,000 JOURNALS

Inspired by such public forms of collaborative, multi-layered communication such as bathroom-wall graffiti and community kiosks, he wondered what would happen if one were to pass around journals, say, 1,000 of them, ask people to write and draw and express themselves in them before sending them on, all the while tracking their progress and ultimately posting the pages on a Web site.

On the 1,000 Journals Web site, he writes: "The idea of passing the journals on can be traced to the Exquisite Corpse, a technique used by Surrealists as a kind of collective collage of words or images... The goal is to provide methods for people to interact and share their creativity."

All 1,000 journals are in circulation, traveling through most of the United States and more than 40 countries worldwide. For more information about the project and to see more journal pages, go to the project Web site at www.1000journals.com.

Reprinted here are images from various journals. They are periodically scanned or photographed by contributors and sent to someguy for posting on the site.

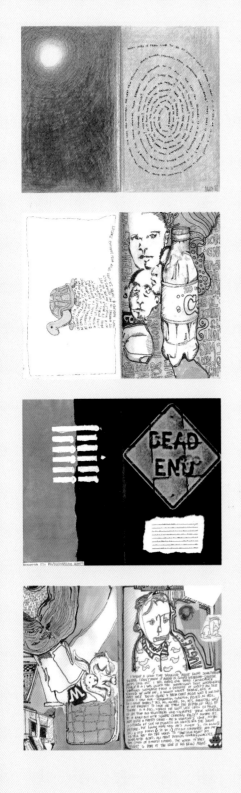

1,000 Journals

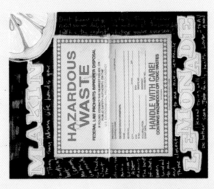

1,000 Journals

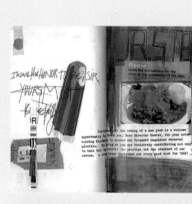

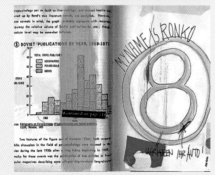

If you're inspired by the idea of collaborating, a round robin might be right for you. To get involved in one, you could:

JOINING A ROUND ROBIN

- **Join** one online. Yahoo's Altered Book list is an easy way to do this. To join, go to http://groups.yahoo.com/group/alteredbooks. The list is also a great resource for talking with artists all over the world, looking at and showing work, and sharing techniques. The one downside to an online round robin is that you won't know much about the other players. Will you like their art? Are they responsible? But if you're willing to embrace the unknown, it's a chance to expand your horizons.

- **Host** one yourself. First, make a plan: How many players can you manage? When and how will books be exchanged? Will there be a general theme? How many spreads will each person do? Then decide if you want to work with artists you know or post an invitation online. Once everyone is onboard, establish an order and timeline, and try to keep to it. As the host, you'll be in charge of making sure everyone is informed and that everything flows. Keep up-to-date by email or phone.

Be prepared for the possibility that a book might get lost, and always make a record of your artwork by photographing, scanning, or photocopying it. You'll want to in any case, because eventually the book will leave your hands. The flipside is that your completed volume will be brimming with wonderful art.

HELGA STRAUSS'S TIPS FOR MAILING ALTERED BOOKS

Protect painted or heavily collaged pages with waxed paper (but let work dry thoroughly—even waxed paper can stick). If a page has fragile elements, pad it with a sheet of bubble wrap. Once it's ready, put the book in a plastic zip bag, wrap it in bubble wrap, and pack it in a sturdy box. Prepare a typed label or write very legibly. Buy insurance and ask others to insure your books. It's worth the extra expense.

What is it that makes a book a book? Is it the rectangular shape, the pages you turn, the fact that it's contained within two covers? Or is it something less tangible, something related more to what a book tells us, the information it holds, and the experience we have when we read or look at it? The books in this chapter—with their multi-tiered pages, unusual shapes, interactive structures, or whimsical narratives—inspire just these sorts of questions and may very well make you pay more attention to how you experience books.

Michael Jacobs describes designing and building the 1990 Kodak Goodwill Games World's Largest

Other Funky Tomes

Photo Album, using (among other materials) plywood, sheet iron, foam padding, and tenting canvas. "While figuring out how to make it work," he says, "I began to see that each massive piece—front and back covers, spine, and book block—was sculptural, yet without much meaning except as a part of the whole book. For the first time, I started to view books as sculptures composed of many parts. It was an exciting discovery." One of his projects here is a multi-paneled pyramid book; instead of turning pages, the reader/viewer disassembles and reassembles it in various formations.

For Karen Michel, the shape or form of a book is not the point as much as it is a gloss on what's inside. *Bird Song*, which features a whimsical series of bird portraits, has a wire-strung cover that evokes a cage. In the house-shaped *Adventures of an Artist*, she rewrites her childhood

story as a myth. It's an intriguing choice to chronicle the journey that is childhood inside a book that's a house. After all, a house is something we generally associate with staying in one place. Somehow, it makes us realize how books are able to move us, both emotionally and figuratively.

Books also move us in another way. Pick up a book and you enter a miniature world created by the writer. The difference with an altered book or artist book is that the world you enter is laid out before your eyes. The richness of the artist's materials, his or her stylistic choices, and the color palettes, all play an important part in how it is experienced. Taking this a step further, Michelle Ward drips scented wax into her altered books and includes special theme-related CDs, engaging not only the mind but also the senses.

At the end of the day, these books are just plain fun. Like the altered books of chapter one, they are made by artists taking joy in the experience of being inside a book, whether they are redreaming a narrative or redefining the parameters of a page. Their enthusiasm gives rise to books that are houses or accordions, books that contain other smaller books—in short, books that are more than the sum of their parts.

Altering a book doesn't have to stop with the pages. While some bindings are already beautiful or interesting, others may be dull or simply not right for your artwork. Luckily, you already have all the resources you need to make a change.

Judging a Book by Its Cover

Janet Hofacker altered the covers shown using funky found objects, paper ephemera, stamps and ink, a craft knife, and a good adhesive. For the small book, she cut a window in the cover, inked the exposed page, and adhered a piece of tag art. She stamped the larger book with letters and added collage elements, including an eye-catching border of dominoes.

Some artists emphasize a book as an object by altering it so that it no longer opens. Rosemary Broton Boyle transformed a book into a shrine by carving a deep niche into the cover (page 92); and Sherrill Hunnibell has done a whole series of books, always using a fixed open spread as her base (pages 102 and 103). Other artists reshape books according to a theme: Karen Michel turned one into a house by cutting it with a saw and applying muffler tape "shingles" to the cover. She turned another into a birdcage by giving its cover a cutout window laced with wire to keep the birds inside. (See page 64 for both.)

Change doesn't always have to be drastic. Simple things like affixing an innovative closure, such as an anchored button with a wrap-around ribbon or a decorative metal clasp, can add charm and character. And keep in mind that unusual materials get extra attention when they appear on the cover: Translucent mica, hand-printed paper, textured fabrics, embossed wallpaper, or metal foils can all be used to great effect.

Artist: Janet Hofacker

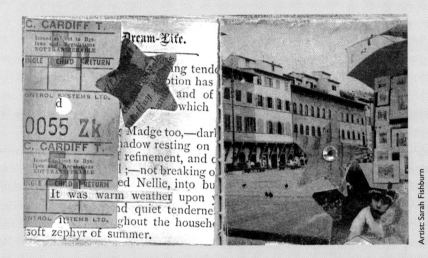

SOME PROJECT IDEAS

Alter a mini: Apply your enthusiasm and skills to a miniature book. The one shown measures 4¹/₄" x 2¹/₂" (10¹/₂ cm x 6 cm) when open. Sarah Fishburn altered the spread using a star punch, rhinestones, acrylic paints, rub-on metallic pigment, and vintage ephemera such as photos, book pages, and a train ticket.

Hide the art: Alter just one or two spreads in a book, then put it back on the shelf or leave it out on your coffee table, waiting to surprise someone.

Book in a box: Cigar boxes, cosmetic compacts, purses, metal tins— any interesting container can hold a book. Turn the box into the binding by removing a book's cover and gluing the block of pages inside the box. Or build a book to fit: Paula Grasdal created an accordion-fold book to lift out of an altered tin. (See page 97.)

Adventures of an Artist and *Bird Song*

Karen Michel

To house her books in something special, Karen Michel created two extraordinary covers using unconventional materials and methods. She shaped the house book with an electric saw, cutting the window with a craft knife. Muffler tape acts as siding, washed with India ink for a patina and "riveted" with upholstery tacks. She laced the window in the bird book with wire to create the impression of a cage. Both projects are filled with colorfully collaged pages that explore, respectively, the themes of childhood and nature.

MATERIALS (for interior pages) photographs and paper ephemera • embellishments such as beads, yarns, feathers, and felt • gesso • watercolor crayons • water-soluble markers • acrylic inks • PVA glue • basic supplies (see page 9)

Karen Michel on beginning "Start off with a children's book or something small in size without hundreds of pages. It's less of a commitment, and you'll have the satisfaction of finishing it in a shorter timeframe. Choose a book with sturdy pages if you plan to work on the actual pages. (Nineteenth-century books tend to have thin, delicate pages that don't handle art materials very well.) Priming your pages with gesso or an acrylic medium first will give them strength and a longer life span."

Altering Photographs To create a dreamy, washed-out effect, the artist primed the pages with gesso and then worked layer by layer with watercolor crayons. She chose photographs reminiscent of her childhood activities and "abused" them with sandpaper, household products, and water-soluble markers, and added text using India ink and a beaten-up pen nib. As you go through your day, be on the lookout for unusual materials—anything with great texture or color that will add character to your piece, no matter how outrageous it may seem, is worth trying out. And hang onto old brushes and pens: They make great mark-making tools.

Working with a Theme Karen Michel populated the pages of *Bird Song* with birds created from collage materials such as maps, feathers, and human eyes cut out from magazines, which give the birds an eerily knowing gaze. Each has a personality based on an ideal or virtue: balance, wisdom, dreamer, guardian angel, etc. By planning out her book in this manner, the artist has provided herself with an opportunity to play with variations on a theme. Consider other thematic approaches: a series of teacups, buildings, or portraits of the same person done in different styles.

Doll-Dress Cut-Out Kit

Jane Maxwell

Doll-dress cutouts come in perfect "one-size-fits-all" packages, sending a message to girls that being tall, thin, and having every dress form-fitted is the desirable norm. To deconstruct this message, Jane Maxwell playfully altered the cutouts and outfits, adorning the figures with exercise charts and lining the dresses with weight-control tips and salad recipes. As a further corrective, she chose basic-but-not-beautiful household materials, such as cardboard, staples, and masking tape, to construct and adorn the pages, along with layer upon layer of beeswax. The spread shown features a pocket, conveniently provided for storing the array of dresses.

MATERIALS paper ephemera such as cutout dolls and dresses, photocopies of original artwork, 1950s housekeeping book pages, fitness charts, vintage blueprints • papers such as vellum, acetate, and cardboard • beeswax • masking tape • staples • sewing machine and thread • basic supplies (see page 9)

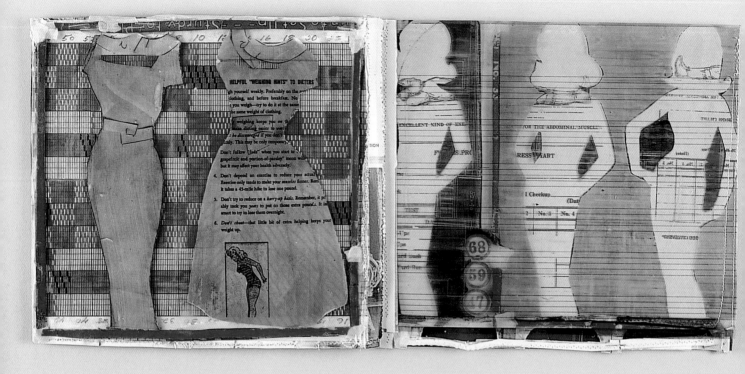

▲ **Adding Subtle Details** When sewing the borders of the pages together, the artist kept the tension on the machine very light to allow loops and excess threads to gather, creating an imperfect line. Keep in mind that even small details such as this can support your book's theme. Each page and dress is covered in layers of beeswax, lending a smooth, preserved-like quality to the pages.

WORKING WITH BEESWAX

Melt the wax in tin cups on a heated palette and use natural bristle brushes (plastic will melt) to apply it in various thicknesses. You can use a blade to carve or smooth certain areas, adding further dimension. Always work in a well-ventilated area, and heat the wax to no more than 220°F (104°C). If it begins to smoke, it is too hot.

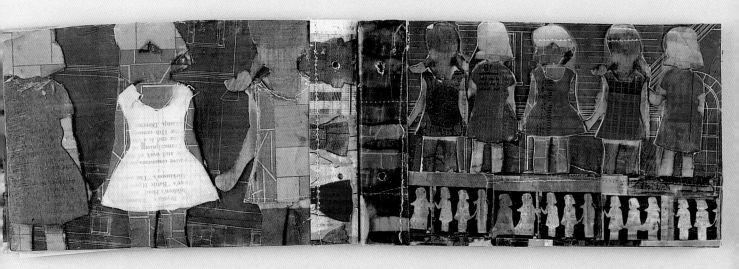

Girls in Dresses

▲ Incorporating Vintage Objects Working in a smaller book format, Maxwell set the figures of young girls against architectural blueprints to suggest how cultural messages about image and dress affect us in formative ways. Throughout the book she uses vintage texts and doll clothes found at flea markets. "Much of my inspiration comes from vintage imagery and objects," she says. "Old items carry an abundance of history, beauty, and often humor—all which I love to incorporate within my art."

Jane Maxwell on book art | "Sometimes it's difficult to tell a story with one piece of art. As most artists do, I often create a series to explore an idea or theme. Book art allows this type of cohesive storytelling in a single, bound form. My book art is essentially a small series that offers a message or tells a story in a unified format."

▲ A simple wire binding with a twist: Doll shoes are attached in front, cardboard doll figures in back. ▼

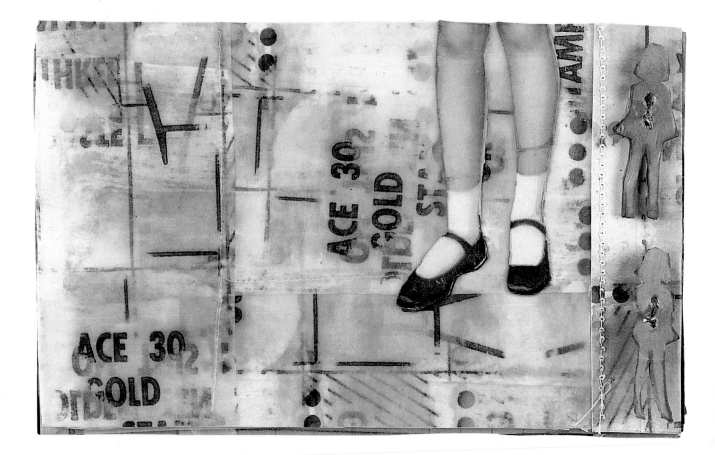

Bookbinding methods and materials are wide-ranging and can be as individual and inventive as the artist book itself. The binding can also enrich the content or character of the work by relating in theme. A nature journal, for example, could be bound with twigs and raffia or a metal book might

Technique Highlight:

CREATIVE BINDING

be fastened with bolts and screws. The bookbinding process often begins with practical considerations, such as how many pages will be fastened and how flat the work should lie when opened. Then the adventure begins! Don't be "bound" by convention—try one of these creative ideas:

• **Tape and other sticky stuff:** Virtually anything that sticks can bind a book. All types of tape—masking, duct, surgical—come in a variety of colors and widths and, adhered vertically or horizontally, add interest while securing pages. Bandages, mailing or filing labels, and contact paper cut into strips of various shapes and sizes are all suitable.

• **Cords, yarns, and ties:** Most traditional methods of bookbinding are based on needle-and-thread stitching patterns and utilize linen thread. Shake it up by sewing with brightly colored yarn, string, raffia, or ribbon. Or use a sewing machine to bind with a zigzag or other interesting stitch. Punch

larger holes, and lace the book together with electrical wire, telephone cord, trash twist ties, measuring tape, a belt, or shoelaces. Strands of beads or chains make a funky alternative.

• **Pins, staples, and screws:** Safety pins, diaper pins, even straight pins will bind a book, and give it a secure look. A household stapler will easily fasten slim volumes. For heavier ones, shoot a staple gun through the book into a sturdy cardboard or wood backing. Nuts and bolts come in all different sizes, have a sleek industrial look, and hold a book together beautifully. Grommets are also great, offering the added benefit of a hole through which to hang charms. Also consider metal rings, which come in many sizes.

• **Buttons and loops:** Binding with buttons is easy and clean. Button the entire book or, if it's too thick, use an alternative method for internal pages and a button-and-loop technique for the front and back covers only. When selecting buttons, search outside the sewing-box for anything that is small and can fit through a hole or loop, such as coins, doll shoes, beads, charms or old wooden bingo numbers...the options are endless. See cords, yarns, and ties above for materials to create cool loops. When securing buttons, be sure to use epoxy or heavy-duty hot glue to keep pieces in place.

—Jane Maxwell

For more information on binding, see *The Handmade Book* by Angela James.

Du Soleil et de la Lune

Mj Viano Crowe

Mj Viano Crowe's bookwork has been shaped over many years of teaching in Paris in January. Without a studio space and renting modest living quarters, she determined she needed to work small. Artist books offered a perfect solution. Inspired by ephemera scavenged from Paris's flea markets, she has created intricately collaged pages from found correspondences, fragments of original poetry with red corrections by a former language professor (such as "no meaning here" and "got a bad feeling"), and reduced photocopies of her own artwork. Her books, with transparent pages that shift their imagery from one composition to the next, allow for discovery through the many hidden elements that are revealed only as the complex, multi-layered, and interactive pages are turned.

MATERIALS black-and-white and color photocopies on paper and acetate • high-quality decorative paper • archival tape • press-type letters •acrylic medium gel • oil of wintergreen (for photo transfers) • waxed thread and upholstery needle • basic supplies (see page 9)

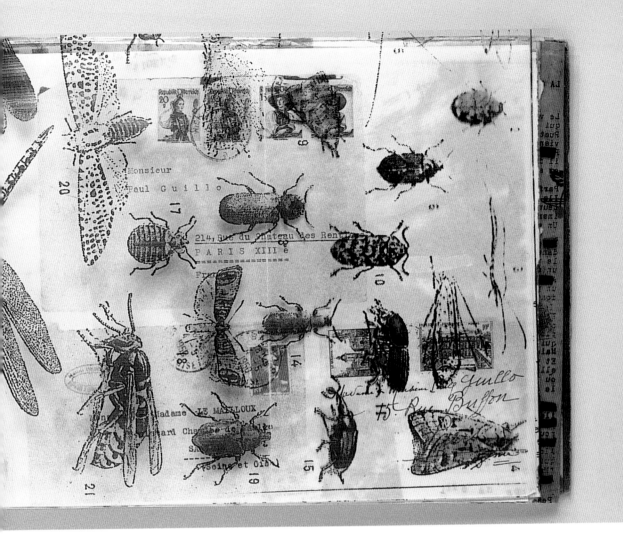

**Mj Viano Crowe
on creating books**

"My books are spiritual journeys as well as oblique journals. Layered with images, opaque and transparent pages both expose and conceal the vulnerable beings I create. Text floats throughout, illuminating voices, history, and the collective unconscious. The nonlinear stories I cobble together are much like a Paris day in January—mystical, romantic, and introspective."

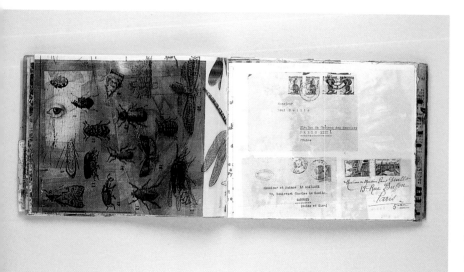

Acetate Layers and Page Extensions Here are two additional views of the spread shown on page 74. The acetate layer is a photocopy of colorful insects, which when turned adds visual complexity on the left and reveals photocopied envelopes on the right. In the envelopes are letters between a British correspondent and a young French woman during the Indochina War; the couple and their life have been richly imagined by the artist. Each envelope page is an extension, securely adhered at the top of the page below. When creating page extensions that fold out, think of hinging them along different margins to vary movement throughout the book and add an element of surprise.

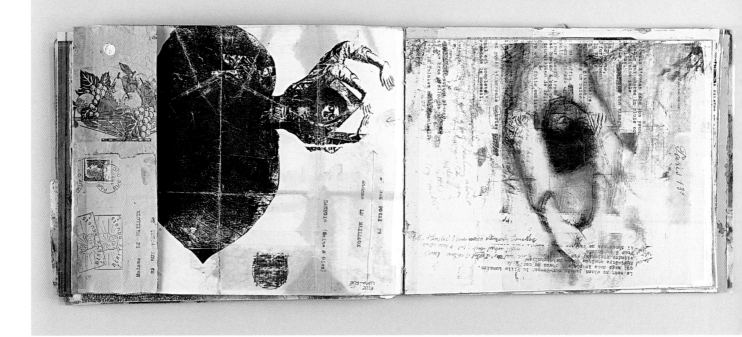

Sampling from Yourself A favorite technique of the artist is to use repeated images—photocopies and transfers of her own art—embellishing them with oil stick, colored pencil, graphite, and text, as shown here. A dancer appears in both spreads as large and small, single and in duplicate. Her raised-arm stance is echoed in the figure of a diver (also repeated). Repeating images in both subtle and direct ways gives a book visual unity while establishing a personal lexicon. It's also a process that leads to unique discoveries as familiar work is made new again by varying the context.

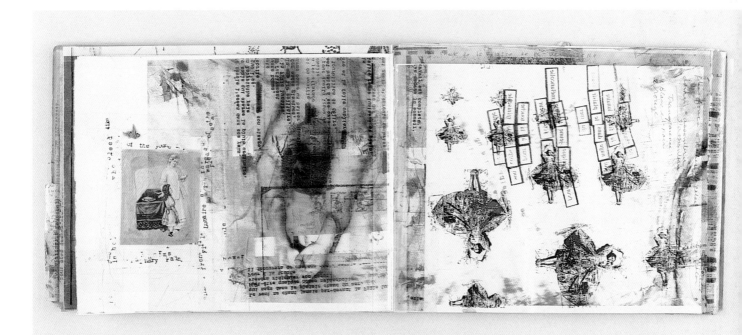

Witness and *Book*

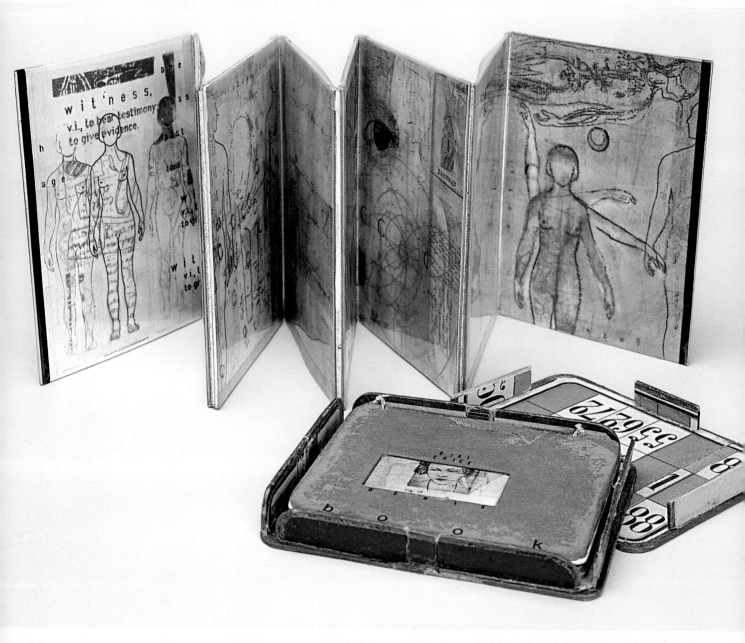

▲ Examples of accordion-fold books by Mj Viano
Crowe: *Witness* (standing) and *Book* (in box).

Book, unfolded from its box. ▶

Not difficult to make yet inherently dramatic, an accordion-fold book can be a satisfying project for a novice book artist. Mj Viano Crowe created two versions, one of which folds away nicely in a box made from old French Lotto cards found at the Porte de Vanves Flea Market in Paris.

Technique Highlight:
ACCORDION-FOLD BOOKS

To make a book like *Book*, cut eight pieces of mat board to size, and glue pairs together to create a thick page. Sand edges to smooth, and then embellish with images, lettering, and photo transfers (see page 27 for various techniques). To attach the panels: Punch holes with an awl, then pull through waxed thread, knotting as you go to hinge each page to the next.

Witness is made in two parts (front and back). For the front, cut and glue seven mat board panels (double-thick) as described above. Embellish with imagery. Photocopy images and text onto acetate and attach to the panels with spray mount adhesive. The acetate layer lets you play with the visuals, adding illusions, shadow figures, and a sense of translucence. For the back, cut a piece of heavy paper that is as wide as the panels are tall and somewhat longer than they are when lying in a row. Embellish as desired. To assemble: Adhere the panels to the paper (acetate facing forward), leaving enough space between them to allow the book to bend. Tape over the fold to strengthen it. Trim excess paper as needed.

A wonderful project for stampers and collage artists, Michelle Ward's house book provides an opportunity to learn about manipulating pages in all kinds of books. By varying page color, transparency,

There's No Place like Home

Michelle Ward

and size, cutting windows to create visual paths through the book, shifting the cut line, and paying attention to how the layers are positioned, you can create a highly interactive book experience. The flexible structure lends itself well to thematic treatments such as childhood memories, family vacations, your dream house, homage to a relationship, or a personal or artistic journey.

MATERIALS cardstock in various colors • decorative vellum • photocopies on acetate • embellishments such as charms, jewels, vintage photographs, paper ephemera • heavy paper for template • binding materials • mini brads, eyelets, wire, and photo corners (for attaching things) • PVA glue • basic supplies (see page 9)

Michelle Ward on capturing the creative muse | "There's nothing like that drive and total energy you have when you start a new project—you're just so full of ideas. What I'll do is get a new scented candle and put on a new CD, and as I'm playing out my new ideas, those things are subliminally happening. I'll actually drip the scented wax right inside my book. So later, recalling that scent or playing that CD takes me immediately back to that excitement I had when I first started."

The key to this project is the double-sided binding, which allows the pages to open like doors. This can work with sewn signatures, coils, or even metal rings (see page 73 for binding alternatives). Create a house-shaped template, then cut assorted papers using a lot of cardstock for stability. Punch holes for binding (or have Kinko's prepare coils). With the pages in order (don't assemble), lightly number with a pencil, marking right- and left-hand corners. Then mark the pages for cutting. Cut the cover down the center, then each consecutive page off-center. Plan ahead, thinking about how the pages relate (i.e., if you want to use a window, place an image beneath it).

▲ Working across Multiple Spreads "In my altered books," says Ward, "one spread is usually across four or six pages, all part of one theme where you can see through to the following pages." Some tips: Add tabs to invite page turning, use envelopes as pages and include poetry or a message, edge pages with decorative tape or paper. The final step is assembly. Choose a method that allows the pages to turn easily and the book to open fully. If using a coil, wind it into the holes and cut it at the bottom so it's one spiral longer than the paper. Twist in and tighten at both ends.

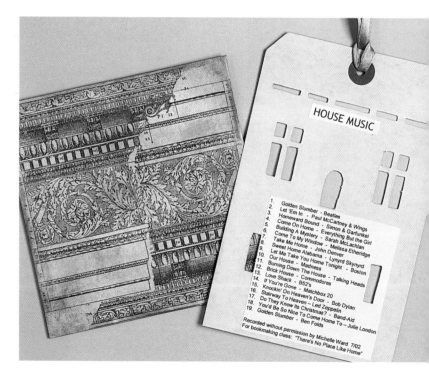

▲ A house is not a home without music, so Ward always makes a theme-related CD to include in her books.

Towers

Michael Jacobs

Measuring a mere ³/₄" (2 cm) thick, this portfolio book sculpture is deceptively slim closed, when it fits as easily into the hand as a paperback novel. Slip off the paper-band closure, and you'll find an accordion-fold book that can stretch its girth to 12" (30 cm) when fully extended. When the book is extended, the towers expose tiny accordion-fold books that unfurl, cascading vertically down the fronts of the towers in an experience that is at once intimate and grand.

MATERIALS embellished cardstock • decorative or embellished papers (for the tiny books) • paper hinges (reinforced with Tyvek) • brass fleur-de-lis • acid-free glue stick • industrial-strength glue (if using a decorative metal element) • basic supplies (see page 9)

Michael Jacobs on books as sculpture

"My book sculptures differ from most collage and other multimedia art in that they are intimate, three-dimensional objects and require the viewer to physically interact with them. I am primarily interested in structure and how things are put together. I am inspired by nature, architecture, art, and viewing handcrafted objects in fiber, wood, clay, metal, and paper. I also get ideas in hardware, kitchen, toy, and import stores, and often see more possibilities in the fixtures than the products."

Triangle Pyramid B·O·O·K

▼ **Exploring Books as Sculpture** Part of a series that explores three- and four-sided triangle structures as both vessel and book, the *Triangle Pyramid B·O·O·K* (shown closed) truly challenges us to think outside the book. Each hinged side incorporates a single section book, and the word "book" is spelled out in numerous ways around the sides and down through the pages. Squares with cut-out centers hold the triangle shape together without tape or glue, allowing for complete flexibility.

▶ **What Is a Page?** In its open position, one can see how the book sculpture can be displayed with various sides upright or lowered to a horizontal position. It can also be reassembled with the inside surfaces on the outside, which allows the word "book" to be spelled backwards in numerous ways around the sides and down through the pages.

▼ **Experimentation and Play** To explore new book forms, cut various shapes out of cardboard or paper and hinge them together in interesting ways with low-tack tape. Use the cutouts as patterns for different materials. "Keep an open mind and be on the lookout for unusual juxtapositions," advises Jacobs. "Experiment with materials that are new to you." Ask yourself how a round book would work or what it means to have pages. Add text to a sheet of paper and let it unfold or unroll from someplace surprising, or write on star-shaped cutouts and cluster them on the front or sides. In the photograph below, the *Triangle Pyramid B•O•O•K* is shown disassembled.

Gallery of Book Pages

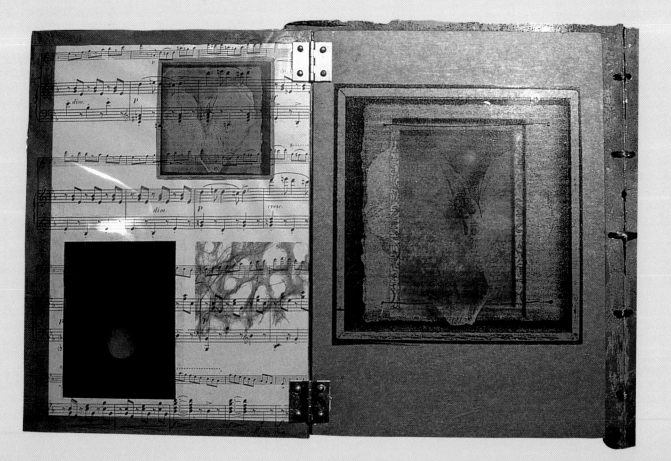

Altered Faces

Judi Riesch

To reinvent an old wooden address book, Judi Riesch substituted vintage photographs for the existing pages, reinforcing the holes with metal washers. Then she used acrylic paints, gel medium, pencils, vintage papers, tintypes, wire mesh, buttons, and beeswax to alter the portraits. She obscured the eyes in some faces, blackening them out completely or veiling them with wire mesh. Riesch prefers to work with actual vintage photographs rather than photocopies because, with their genuine faces captured in time, they provide an intimate connection with the past.

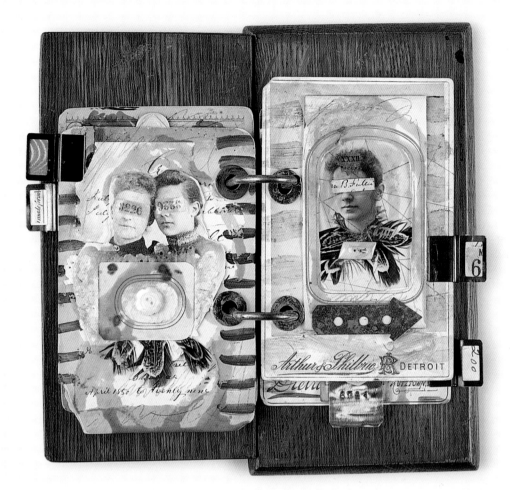

Prayer Time

Rosemary Broton Boyle

Although it looks like a plaster carving, this delicate shrine is really an altered book. Rosemary Broton Boyle cut a deep niche into a vintage hard-cover to expose a preselected page chosen for its interesting text. She ran screws through the book to hold the pages together, and slathered it in wax and paint, embedding the surface with charms, crucifixes, and found objects. A little angel perches at the edge, inviting us to look over its shoulder into the heart of the shrine.

Tweedle Dee

The exterior of this two-panel wooden "book" has been layered with paint, varnish, book pages, and embossed wallpaper. The artist works the materials until they are seamlessly integrated. "I like for people to say, 'How did she do that?'" says Broton Boyle. Here, a raised floral pattern appears to be emerging from the surface, pushing its way through a wall of text.

Homeostasis

Aleta Braun

Begun by Aleta Braun when she returned to school to study reflexology, *Homeostasis* is a fascinating integration of art and science created inside a found journal. For the cover (shown), she used paint, pen and ink, tea bags, paper, a leaf, and encaustic to explore the motif of the "squared circle," representing balance, the union of opposites, and homeostasis, which is the goal of reflexology. As she worked on the pages, she divided the book into chapters, devoting each one to a different system of the body (digestive, reproductive, skeletal, etc.), with all systems being orchestrated by nature's design of homeostasis.

"Foot Comparison" is an interior collage built up around a pencil drawing that compares the feet of two primates (a human and a gorilla). Other elements include found texts from a journal and a book on anatomy. Working intuitively allowed the artist to explore new topics and make connections between the scientific understanding of the world she was confronting

"Foot Comparison"

and what she already knew from living and working in the world as an artist.

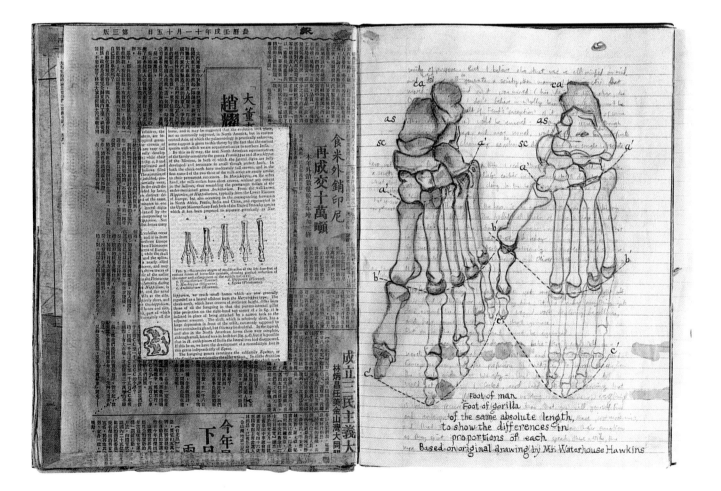

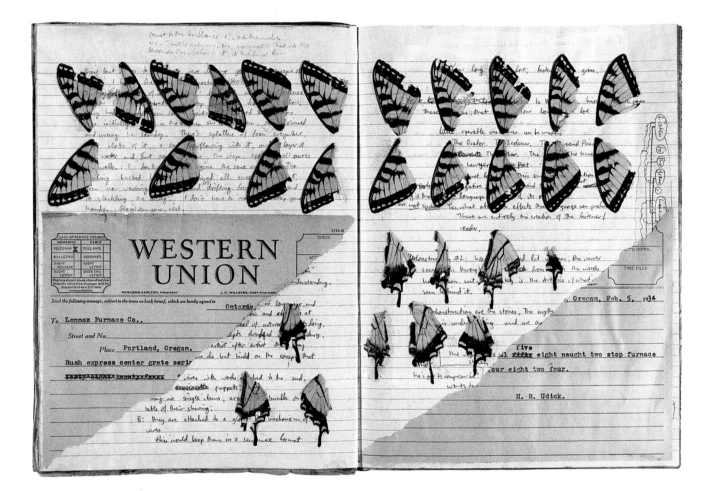

"Western Union"

A telegram with a message about a heating system represents digestive heat and energy, while black and golden swallowtail butterfly wings provide a playful reference to having butterflies in one's stomach. "Making this book balanced my footing when I was very unsure of my ability to comprehend, remember, and coordinate all of this new information," says Braun. "Doing the book made it fun. I would study, study, study, and look forward to my studio time when I could transform all this new information into visual images."

Reflection

Paula Grasdal

Inspired by an old tin discovered at a flea market, Paula Grasdal constructed an accordion-fold book to fit inside using Masonite panels, photocopies on paper and acetate, white mesh, and skeletonized leaf fragments. Diverse media such as dictionary pages, butterfly wings, and black-and-white images of flora are elegantly combined to evoke the feeling of a relic. The book unfolds from the box to reveal a hidden panel, which reflects the viewer's gaze in a tiny mirror.

Red Paris and Maine Journal

John V. Crowe

To create the pages he uses in his artist books, John Crowe layers automatic writings and drawings with found materials and recycled papers, achieving subtle variations in texture and color by sanding, painting, and otherwise transforming the surface. "The dimensions of these works are determined by the size of my pockets," says Crowe. "Small bundles of pages are my constant companions, allowing me to work on café tables, airplane trays, and on small drawing boards I occasionally tie around my neck for long forest hikes."

Pages from the artist book *Maine Journal*.

Unfurl

Laura Friesan

Taking advantage of the implied narrative of books, Laura Friesan arranged memorabilia into an accordion-fold book to create an idiosyncratic visual story. "The format of the book is ideal as it signifies knowledge," she says. "Through sensuous engagement with my books, I hope to open a space to construct individual meanings." The materials she uses—recycled etched metal, glass, natural specimens, and objects such as a braid of hair, a dried orchid, or discarded key—resonate with personal significance. By placing them in a familiar format, she hopes these associations will become accessible to others.

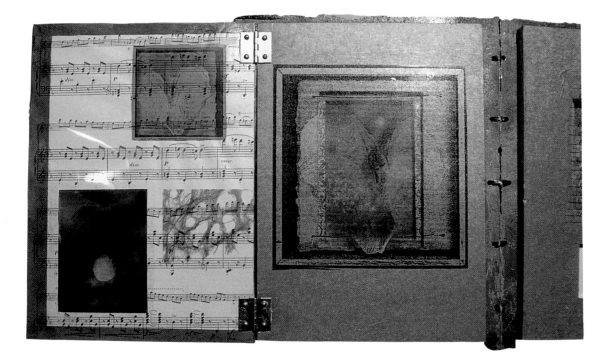

Book of Hours #83: St. Elmo's Fire

Sherrill Hunnibell

The pieces pictured are from Sherrill Hunnibell's *Book of Hours*, a continuing series of mixed-media altered books that reflects her affection for maps, books, and fiber structures, as well as her interest in landscape as both physical space and state of mind. After sealing together the pages to form a base, she creates collages using diverse materials—in this case, copper and brass findings, manipulated found images, papers, acrylic paint and medium, charcoal, and gold leaf—working intuitively in response to the aesthetic interactions of line, shape, color, and texture.

Book of Hours #91:
Untitled Landscape (Purser's Daughter)

Historically, a book of hours was a small daybook used for guidance in meditation. The artist describes her studio time as "a parallel form of meditation achieved through the manipulation of surface and shifts in visual relationships." Here, she has built an abstract landscape out of a purse, leaf, beads, brads, computer components, industrial findings, manipulated found images, a map, acrylic paint and medium, charcoal, and gold leaf. Through a complex process of layering and excavating the surface, she has created a harmonious whole.

Nine Triangle Ritual Books

Michael Jacobs

Michael Jacobs constructed these books as part of an ongoing series that explores three- and four-sided triangle structures as both vessel and book. His books are completely interactive: The sides are held together with wooden dowels and/or paper toppers that, when removed, allow the viewer to reposition the book at will. Small books are variously attached to the outside, housed within, or integrated into the sides of the structures.

Photography: Bill Wickett

On Foot

Kerrie Carbary

Kerrie Carbary created *On Foot* over the course of two years as an exploration of journeying and soul-searching. She altered the pages using acrylic paints, gold leaf, watercolor, ink, water-soluble crayons, collage, handwritten text, found objects, and sewn lines. This spread features multiple cutouts: A window shows the page below while the spaces between the fence bars have been cut away to create an overlay effect with the next page. The imagery and approach evoke the feeling of the open road and its possibilities.

Here is another example of the artist's multi-layered, highly textured approach. Much of the page below—with its layer of gold transparent fabric, ink work, and stitching—is visible as part of the composition, as scraps of original text, and the painted edges of other pages. Seeming to emerge from the page is the image of a child clown, a black-and-white photocopy rubbed with paint. A sewn diagonal line increases the tactile nature of the surface, with the same metallic thread used to stitch the edges of several pages.

"I like shaping the content of the book like a sculpture," says Carbary, "finding the words and images that I want to pull to the front, and adding my own to create a meaningful piece. I actually like the limitations of working in the altered book format. The existing book gives a structure that I might not necessarily have chosen, which challenges me in ways that help me grow as an artist."

"Andros"

Rhonda Roebuck

An old ledger that had been used for medical notes provided the base for Rhonda Roebuck's book and became a laboratory for exploring themes that interested her. Here she used water-soluble crayons to embellished photographs taken by her husband while he was in Andros, in the Bahamas. "The underwater photos he takes always look like little paintings to me," she says. "They have an ethereal, surreal quality." After adhering the photos in place, she enhanced that effect by working the page with paint and crayons to blend the line between photograph and page.

Photography: Bill Moritz

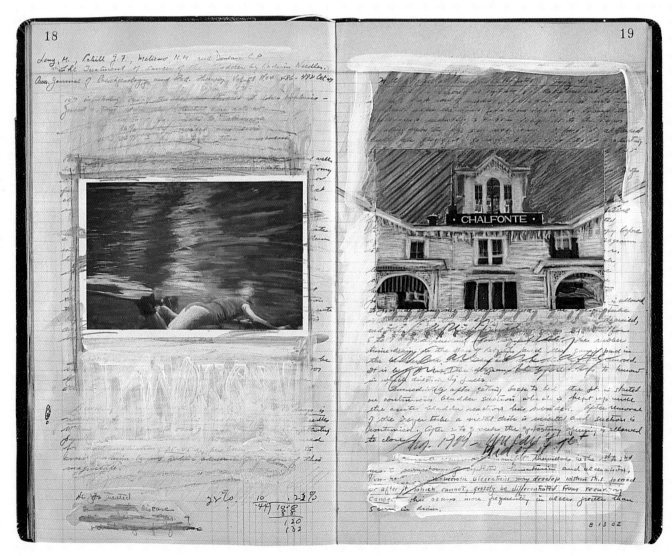

Photography: Bill Moritz

"Sweetwater, Tennessee"

Intrigued by photographs of women in her family no one can identify, Roebuck created a kind of homage. She integrated the visual elements with the medical notations by washing the pages with acrylic paint, collaging on found text, and adding photo transfers of the women and a pair of beautiful vintage spoons. The effect is evocative and mysterious, as if the women are floating in a wash of memory.

Charlotte's Web

When Livia McRee altered *Charlotte's Web*, one of her favorite children's books, the first thing she did was correct a gross oversight: She added Templeton, the rat, to the cover, where as a major player he should have been all along. She also personalized the story with images of other animals in her life. One of these animals, Dale, an adopted pig now living at a farm sanctuary, has been immortalized with a small color-pencil portrait (not shown).

Livia McRee

The artist added a few fanciful touches to the endpapers: glitter glue and torn-up tissue paper featuring images of pigs. The kaleidoscopic effect is a whimsical embellishment that also serves to emphasize the stickiness associated with a spider's web. In other parts of the book, she used linen hinging tape and mulberry paper to attach long, colorfully painted extensions.

Working in an old Russian textbook altered to be about lesser-known female photographers, Sarah Fishburn created this graphic spread using vintage and personal photos, handmade papers, text, rub-on metallic pigment, star brads, and assorted collage elements. She found herself inspired by photographer Tina Modotti's struggle to integrate her artistic life and political ideals. To make a connection to her own life and concerns, she included parallel photographs: one, a beach scene taken by Modotti, and the other a beach shot of the artist's daughter, Sierra-Marie, as a child.

Fun and Revolution

Sarah Fishburn

"Spin Me"

Helga Strauss

Helga Strauss received her inspiration for altering this dictionary page from a vintage postcard with a rotating cardboard clock dial. She adapted the idea, substituting a CD for the cardboard dial and collaging it with images. She then altered the page as shown, cutting a window and attaching the CD behind it. Spinning the disc reveals different women inside the house.

Nina Bagley altered a vintage book as a gift for a pregnant friend. She reconstructed the pages using trinkets and found objects (attached with eyelets and wire), gilded fabrics, and mica to add sparkle, and altered vintage photographs into depictions of fanciful insect girls and angels. Every page provides a new revelation, with personal messages and advice for the baby tucked into envelopes and under flaps, and fragments of poetry celebrating childhood scattered throughout.

Untitled Baby Book

Nina Bagley

When she first started this project, Bagley told her friend she was making a traditional baby book with lots of blank space for recording special events and baby data. "I just couldn't do it," she confesses. "I kept filling in those pages myself with art, and even had to *re-do* the original binding to expand it and make it wider for all the thick pages. She finally got the book about a month before Maggie was born, with very few blank pages! Hence, the tiny blank altered book in the back."

Deborah Putnoi gave new life to a library discard by painting and collaging in it until she had reinvented every page. Although she obscured much of the text with artwork, she also highlighted some of the words, adding nuance to the visual themes. "My work is an attempt to understand my interior landscape of thoughts, perceptions, fears, and questions," she says. Consequently, the book evokes a sense of exploration and discovery through the juxtaposition of personal writings and intimate line drawings against random elements such as phone book pages, torn and cut-up drawings, and fabric scraps.

Thinking Me

Deborah Putnoi

Working in preprinted books has proven to be a fruitful experience for Putnoi. "Having something already on the page is inspiring," she says. "It's something to work against. Layering images, materials, and my own text on an existing structure, I push past the intended meaning and use of a book and make it my own." Here, she has added a scrap of poem, a phone book page, and multiple layers of paint and drawing.

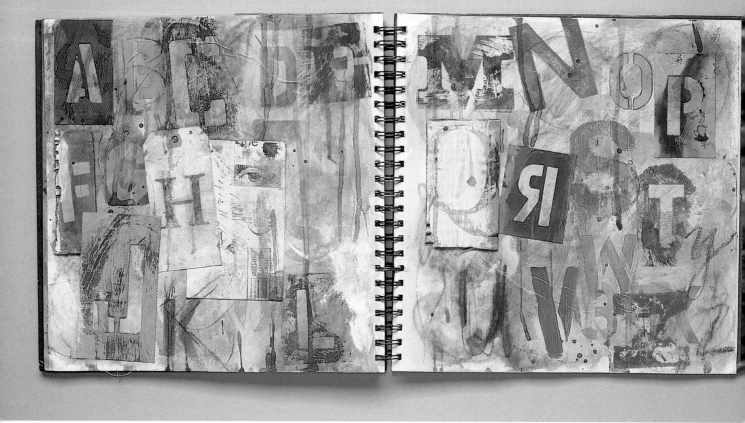

These journal pages by Lynne Perrella are a rendition of an alphabet and are part of a series of journal explorations on the subject. To make this colorful and graphic spread, she used acrylic paints, cardboard stencils, mono printing, and collage, creating the impression of a book dipped into various vats of color. "As mixed-media artists, we have an affinity for tactile, hands-on expression," says Perrella, "and it was only a matter of time before we began to think of an entire book as a collage element."

Untitled Journal Page

Lynne Perrella

Wings

Lisa Vollrath

Lisa Vollrath's colorful project *Wings* is an example of how an artist can find plenty to challenge her, even in a simple children's book. This one offered a fun shape and the visual punch of a pop-up element on each page, which had to be incorporated into the new design. To alter the cover, she added a layer of watercolor paper, some laser-printed letters, and a plastic lizard with shrink-plastic wings.

After obscuring the text with hand-painted cloud paper, the artist revamped
these pages into a playful reference to how "time flies." The watches are
rubber-stamped images applied to metallic papers, with wings made of laser
prints or fabric. This spread follows one covered with collaged butterflies (not
shown) and precedes another (page 121) in which wings are worn by a hand-
painted scarab (done with glass paints) and a representation of the goddess Isis.

Lisa Vollrath advises beginners to "ignore what everyone tells you and just dive in. Don't sit around and think about it, and don't make it complicated. Just find an old book and start making art. Use whatever skills you have—if you're a stamper, start stamping. If you paint, start painting. When people tell me, 'I haven't altered a book yet,' my response is always, 'What the heck are you waiting for?'"

Product Resource Guide

This guide is organized by project and by vendor. Look under the selected projects below to find out about the particular products and materials used, and then consult the vendor listing for more information.

Projects

Chapter One: Altered Books

Page 14: *Become Me* by Brenda Murray

Neutral pH Adhesive by Lineco, fluid acrylic paints by Golden, and Lettering by Letraset are available at art supply stores.

Waxed linen thread for bookbinding is available at paper stores.

Images from Dover Books.

Page 24: *a birdlike heart* by LK Ludwig

Chartpak blenders and superblack India ink by Speedball are available at art and craft supply stores.

Copper topper paint and patina green solution are made by Modern Options.

Procion dyes are available at Dharma Trading Company and art supply stores.

Page 34: *The Optimist's Good Night, Pond,* and *Finds* by Sharon McCartney

Knox gelatin is available at grocery stores.

Rice paper, Rives BFK, and Speedball water-soluble inks are available at art supply or paper stores.

Chapter Two: Collaborations

Page 42: "She Had No Paper for Drawing" by Sarah Fishburn

Coccoina glue sticks are available at Anima Designs.

Page 46: "Little Red Riding Hood" and "Little Seamstress" by Jill S. Haddaway

Ancient Page sandalwood ink by Colorbox is available at art supply stores.

Page 48: "Let's Play Dress Up" by Karenann Young

Rubber stamps from ARTchix Studio, Zettiology, and Acey Deucy.

Color image from ARTchix Studio.

Page 48: "Come Fly with Me" by Karenann Young

Rubber stamps and color image from ARTchix Studio.

Page 50: "Marseillaise" and "She Wanted to Go to Paris" by Kristin Ashton

Acrylic paints and acrylic matte medium by Golden and Metallic inkpads by Colorbox are available at art supply stores.

Hot-press watercolor paper by Fabriano is available at art supply or paper stores.

Transparency film for inkjet printers by Appollo is available at Office Depot.

Page 52: "She Plays" by Helga Strauss

Collage sheet images from ARTchix Studio.

Page 54: "Parrucche 1800–1900" and "Très Groovy" by Cathleen Perkins

Archival glue stick by Uhu and permanent inkpad by Memories are available at art and craft supply stores.

Chapter Three: Other Funky Tomes

Page 62: Judging a Book by Its Cover

Inks available at Clearsnap Inc.

Acrylic paints from Plaid Enterprises Inc.

Adhesive: Yes! Glue, Call (800) 521-4263 for distributors.

Page 64: *Adventures of an Artist* and *Bird Song* by Karen Michel

Portfolio Series water-soluble oil pastels are manufactured by Crayola.

Muffler tape is available at auto supply stores and Home Depot.

Page 74: *Du Soleil et de la Lune* by Mj Viano Crowe

Filmoplast P archival tape and acetate pages are available at Light Impressions.

Page 80: *There's No Place like Home* by Michelle Ward

Coil binders and coils (in various colors) are available at Bonnie's Best Art Tools.

A house kit, which includes instructions, template, and basic papers, can be purchased from the artist. For more info, go to www.greenpepperpress.com or see Artist Directory (page 126).

Page 84: *Towers* and *Triangle Pyramid B•O•O•K* by Michael Jacobs

Tyvek: You can buy Tyvek envelopes at the post office or office supply stores, then cut project pieces to size. It is manufactured in different thicknesses. #1085D Tyvek (nice and thick) is available at Matthias Paper Corp.

Vendors

Please contact the vendors below for information on the products listed as well as other art supplies.

North America

Acey Deucy
P.O. Box 194
Ancram, NY 12502
complete catalog: $5.00
rubber stamps

A.C. Moore craft stores
See www.acmoore.com for store locations
art and crafts supplies

Anima Designs

www.animadesigns.com
rubber stamps, bookmaking supplies, and ephemera

ARTchix Studio

1957 Hampshire Road
Victoria, BC,
Canada V8R 5T9
phone: (250) 370-9985
fax: (250) 370-0985
www.artchixstudio.com
helga@artchixstudio.com
collage sheets with vintage images, transparencies, fabric, rubber stamps, accessories, and embellishments

Bonnie's Best Art Tools

Atlanta, GA
phone: (404) 869-0081
www.coilconnection.com
coil binders, coils, eyelet punches, book drills, and other tools for binding

Clearsnap Inc.

P.O. Box 98
Anacortes, WA 98221
phone: (800) 448-4862
www.clearsnap.com
inkpads and rubber stamps

Coffee Break Design

P.O. Box 34281
Indianapolis, IN 46234
phone: (317) 290-1542
wholesale supplier of brads, eyelets, embellishments, art supplies

Colophon Book Arts Supply

3611 Ryan Street SE
Lacey, WA 98503
phone: (360) 458-6920
mail-order bookbinding supplies, decorative papers, marbling supplies

Dakota Art Store Ltd.

6110 Roosevelt Way NE
Seattle, WA 98115
phone: (206) 523-4830
papers and art supplies

Daniel Smith Inc.

4150 First Avenue S.
Seattle, WA 98134
phone: (206) 223-9599
www.danielsmith.com
papers and art supplies

de Medici Ming Fine Paper

1222 First Avenue, #A
Seattle, WA 98101
phone: (206) 624-1983
handmade specialty papers

Dharma Trading Company

www.dharmatrading.com
online source of textile craft supplies

Dick Blick Art Materials

phone (for catalog):
(800) 723-2787
www.dickblick.com
mail-order art and crafts supplies

Hollander's

407 North Fifth Street
Ann Arbor, MI 48104
phone: (734) 741-7531
www.hollanders.com
decorative papers, bookbinding supplies, book cloth, and workshops

Home Depot

See www.homedepot.com
for store locations

Ichiyo Art Center

432 Paces Ferry Road
Atlanta, GA 30305
phone: (800) 535-2263
www.ichiyoart.com
Japanese papers, origami supplies, and rubber stamps

Japanese Paper Place

887 Queen Street W
Toronto, ON
Canada M6J1G5
phone: (416) 703-0089
www.interlog.com
Japanese washi and other decorative papers

John Neal Bookseller

1833 Spring Garden Street
Greensboro, NC 27403
phone: (800) 369-9598
www.JohnNealBooks.com
books on calligraphy, book arts, and supplies for calligraphers and book artists

Kinko's

See www.kinkos.com for
store locations

Light Impressions

phone: (800) 828-6216
www.lightimpressions
direct.com
archival, scrapbooking, and photo supplies

Matthias Paper Corp.

301 Arlington Boulevard
Swedesboro, NJ 08085
phone: (800) 523-7633
Tyvek and other paper supplies

Ma Vinci's Reliquary

P.O. Box 472702
Aurora, CO 80047
www.crafts.dm.net/mall/
reliquary
alphabet rubber stamps

Michaels

See www.michaels.com
for store locations
art and crafts supplies

Modern Options

www.modernoptions.com
rust and patina kits, metallics, primers, accessories

Office Depot

See www.officedepot.com
for store locations

Paper and Ink Arts

3 North Second Street
Woodsboro, MD 21798
phone: (800) 736-7772
www.PaperInkArts.com
inks, pens, tools, books, and papers for calligraphers and book artists

Paper Source

See www.paper-source.com
for store locations in
California, Illinois,
Massachusetts, Missouri,
and Minnesota
decorative and handmade papers, bookmaking supplies, and workshops

Paper-Ya

9-1666 Johnston Street
Vancouver, BC
Canada V6H 3S2
handmade and specialty papers

Pearl Paint Company

308 Canal Street
New York, NY 10013
phone: (800) 451-PEARL
(for catalog)
art and crafts supplies

Plaid Enterprises Inc.

3225 Westech Drive
Norcross, GA 30092
phone: (800) 842-4197
acrylic paints, rubber stamps, and other craft supplies

Portfolio Series Water-Soluble Oil Pastels

www.portfolioseries.com
or www.crayola.com

R&F Handmade Paints

506 Broadway
Kingston, NY 12401
phone: (800) 206-8088
www.rfpaints.com
high-quality encaustic paints and pigment sticks

Rugg Road Paper Company

105 Charles Street
Boston, MA 02114
phone: (617) 742-0002
handmade specialty papers and bookmaking workshops

Seattle Art Supply

2108 Western Avenue
Seattle, WA 98121
phone: (206) 625-0711
www.seattleartsupply.com
papers and art supplies

Stampington Company

www.stampington.com
rubber stamps and related supplies

Strathmore Artist Papers

www.strathmoreartist.com
for suppliers

Turtle Press

2215 NW Market Street
Seattle, WA 98107
www.turtlearts.com
specialized paper arts supplies, rubber stamps, alphabet rubber stamps, and other useful items for altered book artists

Twinrocker Handmade Paper

phone: (800) 757-8946
twinrocker@twinrocker.com

Utrecht Art

phone: (800) 223-9132
See www.utrechtart.com
for store locations or to order online
art supplies

Zettiology

P.O. Box 3329
Renton, WA 98056
fax: (425) 271-5506
www.zettiology.com;
catalog: $4
(also available online)
rubber stamps and mythos

Europe and United Kingdom

Creative Crafts

11 The Square
Winchester
Hampshire, UK SO23 9ES
phone: 01962 856266
www.creativecrafts.co.uk
art and craft supplies

Graphi Gro

11 arrondisement
Paris, France
art supplies

Gilbert-Jean Booksellers

Lower Level
Left Bank
Paris, France
art supplies

HobbyCraft

(stores throughout the UK)
Head Office
Bournemouth, England
phone: 1202 596 100
art and craft supplies

John Lewis

Oxford Street
London, England
W1A 1EX
phone: 207 629 7711
See www.johnlewis.co.uk
for store locations throughout the UK
department store with art and craft supplies

Paris Flea Markets

Clingancourt

Metro stop: Pte de
Clingancourt
hours: Sat, Sun, Mon
(all day)

Porte de Vanves

Metro stop: Pte de Vanves
hours: Sat, Sun (early morning until noon)

Porte de Montreuil

Metro stop: Pte de
Montreuil
hours: Sat, Sun, Mon
(all day)

Australia and New Zealand

Bondi Road Art Supplies

179–181 Bondi Road
Bondi, NSW 2026
phone: (612) 9387 3746
www.bondiroadart.com.au
pigments, paints, paper, books, inks, canvases, brushes

Eckersley's Arts, Crafts, and Imagination

phone (for catalog):
1-300-657-766
See www.eckersleys.com.au
for store locations in New South Wales, Queensland, South Australia, and Victoria
art and craft supplies

Main Art

See www.mainart.co.nz
for store locations throughout New Zealand
art supplies and handmade papers

Additional Resources

The Center for Book Arts, New York City

www.centerforbookarts.org

A nonprofit organization dedicated to preserving the craft of bookmaking and encouraging contemporary interpretations of the book as an art object.

International Society of Altered Book Artists

www.alteredbook.com/
internationalsocietyof
alteredbookartists.htm

An international nonprofit organization dedicated to promoting book altering as an art form.

Yahoo Altered Books list

http://groups.yahoo.com/
group/altered books

An international online forum for altered book artists; also a good resource for locating altered book groups in different parts of the world.

Bibliography and Additional Reading

Bibliography

ARTitude Zine. Issues 1 to 4 (Summer, Autumn, and Winter 2001; Spring 2002)

Cote, Beth and Cindy Pestka. *Altered Books 101.* Ft. Worth, TX: Design Originals, 2002.

dog eared magazine. Issue 3 (Summer 2001). Seattle, WA: Turtle Press.

James, Angela. *The Handmade Book.* North Adams, MA: Storey Books, 2000.

LaPlantz, Shereen. *Cover to Cover: Creative Techniques for Making Beautiful Books, Journals & Albums.* New York: Lark Books, 2000.

Lauf, Cornelia and Clive Phillpot. *Artist/Author: Contemporary Artists' Books.* New York: Distributed Art Publishers, 1998.

Sackner, Marvin. *The Altered Page* (exhibition catalog). New York: Book Arts Gallery, 1988.

Recommended Reading

Carbary, Kerrie. *Altered Art Books.* Seattle, WA: Turtle Press, January 2003.

Drucker, Johanna. *Figuring the Word: Essays on Books, Writing, and Visual Poetics.* New York: Granary Books, 1998.

Ely, Tim. *The Flight into Egypt.* San Francisco: Chronicle Books, 1995.

Philipps, Tom. *Works and Texts.* London: Thames and Hudson, 1992.

Thompson, Jason. *Making Journals By Hand.* Gloucester, MA: Rockport Publishers, 2000.

Recommended Zines That Feature Altered Books and Art Journals:

art-e-zine (www.art-e-zine.co.uk); *ARTitude Zine* (www.artitudezine.com); *dog eared magazine* (www.dogearedmagazine.com); *Play* and *The Studio* (www.teeshamoore.com).

Of note: The Book of Zines at www.zinebook.com is a site devoted to zines, with contact information, a history of zines, and tips on starting your own.

Artist Directory

Kristin Ashton

Kirkland, WA
KLUVSPARIS@aol.com
www.outofthebluestudio
.com

Nina Bagley

796 Savannah Drive
Sylva, NC 28779
papernina@aol.com
www.itsmysite.com/
ninabagleydesign

Aleta Braun

302 South Library Street
Greenville, NC 27858
aletabob@earthlink.net

Rosemary Broton Boyle

Artists West Association
144 Moody Street
Waltham, MA 02453
studio phone:
(781) 736-0299
paintrmom@aol.com

Kerrie Carbary

P.O. Box 17545
Seattle, WA 98107
www.turtlearts.com

publisher of *dog eared
magazine*: www.dogeared
magazine.com

John V. Crowe

Massachusetts College
of Art
621 Huntington Avenue
Boston, MA 02115
jcrowe@massart.edu

Sarah Fishburn

Fort Collins, CO
sarah_fishburn@yahoo.com
or gerety@verinet.com
www/frii.com/~gerety/
SarahFishburn

Laura Friesan

Vancouver, BC, Canada
phone: (604) 255-2363
lfriesan@telus.net

Paula Grasdal

Cambridge, MA
paulagrasdal@earthlink.net

Jill S. Haddaway

Seattle, WA
jill-the-reckless@attbi.com
www.weeladstudio.com

Janet Hofacker

Sherrill Hunnibell

Rehoboth, MA

Michael Jacobs

The Creative Zone
P.O. Box 19458
Seattle, WA 98109
creativezone@earthlink.net
www.thecreativezone.com

LK Ludwig

P.O. Box 103
Slippery Rock, PA 16057
lorikay.ludwig@sru.edu

Jane Maxwell

Newton, MA
janemaxwell@attbi.com

Sharon McCartney

Lexington, MA
LilyPeek@aol.com

**Melissa McCobb
Hubbell**

14 Rochambeau Avenue
Ridgefield, CT 06877
mmhubbell@earthlink.net
www.melissamccobb
hubbell.com

Livia McRee

Livia@liviamcree.com
www.liviamcree.com

Karen Michel

phone: (516) 897-3859
kmichelny@hotmail.com
www.karenmichel.com

Brenda Murray

Montreal, Quebec, Canada
bmurray@equilibre.biz
www.brendamurray.net

Lynne Perrella

Ancram, NY
www.LKPerrella.com

Judi Riesch

Philadelphia, PA
JJRiesch@aol.com
www.itsmysite.com/
judiriesch

Rhonda Roebuck

Greenwood, VA
www.cstone.net/~fmb4p/
webart/Rhonda.html

Suz Simanaitis

Los Angeles, CA
saucydivadesign@aol.com
www.saucydiva.com

co-publisher of
ARTitude Zine:
www.artitudezine.com

Helga Strauss

Victoria, BC, Canada
phone: (250) 370-9985
helga@artchixstudio.com
ARTchix Studio Web site:
www.artchixstudio.com

co-publisher of
ARTitude Zine:
www.artitudezine.com

Cathleen Perkins

Bozeman, MT
cath@in-tch.com
www.karststage.com/
artdreams

Deborah Putnoi

Belmont, MA
artforachange@aol.com

Mj Viano Crowe

Department of Fine Arts
Stonehill College
Easton, MA 02357
phone: (508) 565-1168
mvcrowe@stonehill.edu

Lisa Vollrath

Euless, TX
www.lisavollrath.com

Michelle Ward

Piscataway, NJ
GRNPEP@optonline.net
www.greenpepperpress.com

Karenann Young

www.picturetrail.com/
karenannyoung

**1,000 Journals
Project**

someguy@1000journals.com
www.1000journals.com

About the Author

Holly Harrison is a freelance writer and editor. Previous books include: *Angel Crafts: Graceful Gifts and Inspired Designs for 47 Projects* and *Collage for the Soul: Expressing Hopes and Dreams through Art* (coauthored with Paula Grasdal). She has contributed artwork to her own books as well as to Kathy Cano-Murillo's *Making Shadow Boxes and Shrines*.

I would like to thank the usual suspects at Rockport for their hard work in putting together the book: Silke Braun, Sarah Chaffee, Cora Hawks, David Martinell, Kristy Mulkern, and Winnie Prentiss. Thanks also to Bobbie Bush for her wonderful photography. A special thank-you is reserved for my editor, Mary Ann Hall, for her guidance and friendship.

Acknowledgments

It should be noted that the artists' contributions go far beyond their individual projects. Much of my research was based on phone and email interviews and studio visits. All were incredibly generous with their time, answering my many questions and enthusiastically sharing their insights on books and art.

Paula Grasdal helped by reading the manuscript while it was still wobbly and offering keen editorial feedback. Thanks, too, to my husband, Jim McManus, for being my sounding board and late-night dinner companion.

Early on, I wrote to Lynne Perrella, and to my delight she responded with an avalanche of emails filled with artist names, book titles, and some of her thoughts on art and life. I am grateful to her for her assistance.

Numerous people helped in the search for artists by steering me to Web sites, books, and magazines. They include Patti Culea, Jill K. Jones, Pat Price, and many of the artists.

Finally, this book is dedicated to the artists featured on its pages. Their generosity and talent has made it possible.